28 JOBS, 28 WEEKS, 28 STATES

Jubanashwa Mishra

SPEAKING TIGER BOOKS LLP
125A, Ground Floor, Shahpur Jat, near Asiad Village,
New Delhi 110049

This edition published by Speaking Tiger Books 2022

Copyright © Jubanashwa Mishra 2022

This book is about my real experiences—except in a few cases where I have taken literary license with fictional twists to make the actual events more dramatic. During the course of 28 jobs in 28 weeks through 28 states I interacted with many people from different walks of life, and the book is peppered with them. Some of the names have been changed to protect identities.

ISBN: 978-93-5447-170-4
eISBN: 978-93-5447-178-0

10 9 8 7 6 5 4 3 2 1

Typeset in Arno Pro by SÜRYA, New Delhi
Printed at HT Media Ltd, Greater Noida

All rights reserved.
No part of this publication may be reproduced, transmitted, or stored in a retrieval system, in any form or by any means, electronic, mechanical, photocopying, recording or otherwise, without the prior permission of the publisher.

This book is sold subject to the condition that it shall not, by way of trade or otherwise, be lent, resold, hired out, or otherwise circulated, without the publisher's prior consent, in any form of binding or cover other than that in which it is published.

Jubanashwa Mishra was born in Sonepur in western Odisha. A district topper at school, he did his higher studies in the nearest big town, Sambalpur. After graduating in Engineering, he joined Tata Consultancy Services where he worked for three years, before joining the MICA School for Ideas, Ahmedabad, for a post-graduate degree.

Before starting his adventurous '28 Jobs' journey Jubanashwa worked on many challenging projects ranging from digital consulting for top companies, to the biggest rural brand activation through folk-theatre, a first-time-ever initiative.

He embarked on his project of doing 28 jobs in 28 weeks in all the 28 states of India, in May 2013, and completed his journey in December the same year. During this time, he did a variety of jobs, ranging from being a mountain cleaner to a tattoo maker, a rafting trainee and even an assistant in a crematorium!

He currently lives in Bhubaneswar where he runs his own gaming startup called Paperboat Labs.

Married to a Bengali, he loves eating fish fry along with his comfort Odia dish, Pakhala. Apart from storytelling, his passions are movies, books and travelling.

To my parents
Thank you for being there for me—and for all the comforts of home whenever I was broke!

Contents

Acknowledgements	xi
Prologue	1
1. Gujarat *Cheers to Single Malt in a 'Dry State'!*	13
2. Rajasthan *My First Encounter with World Travellers*	23
3. Himachal Pradesh *Cleaning Hillsides with the Waste Warriors*	35
4. Punjab *Seva and Langar at the Golden Temple*	48
5. Jammu & Kashmir *The Waters that Almost Swept Me to Pakistan*	59
6. Uttarakhand *Within Miles of Devastating Floods*	71
7. Haryana *Capturing Ethnic Weaves on Camera*	80

8. Maharashtra   87
A Taste of Bollywood with the Lootera Stars

9. Goa   101
Each Tattoo Has a Story to Tell

10. Karnataka   120
Assisting an Emotion Management Counsellor

11. Tamil Nadu   127
Selling Peanuts on Marina Beach

12. Kerala   134
Steering a Houseboat Through the Backwaters

13. Andhra Pradesh   141
Dealing with Toddlers' Tantrums at a Playschool

14. Odisha   148
Spending a Week in My Own State—Far From Home

15. Chhattisgarh   156
Content Writing for Job Aspirants

16. Jharkhand   160
Discovering Jamshedpur Through Data Entry and on Foot

17. Bihar   165
Selling Condoms in Rural India

18. Uttar Pradesh   176
Cremation Sites, Aghoris and Their Reality

19. West Bengal   187
From the Potter's Wheel to Bolting from Sonagachi

20. Assam — 195
Learning the Ropes at a Tea Factory

21. Sikkim — 203
Tossing Mojitos at a Gangtok Bar

22. Arunachal Pradesh — 210
Storytelling with Little Monks at Tawang Monastery

23. Nagaland — 219
No Job Vacancies for Strangers in a Gun House

24. Manipur — 226
The Indian Army, AFSPA and the Citizens

25. Tripura — 235
Launching a Portal with Student Entrepreneurs

26. Mizoram — 240
Bike Mechanic by Day, Insurgency History at Night

27. Meghalaya — 249
Working Among HIV+ People in Shillong

28. Madhya Pradesh — 256
From a Real Estate Firm to Dhuandhar Falls

Epilogue — 262

In Gratitude — 265

Acknowledgements

This book is the outcome of an experience of a lifetime, an exploration, a leap of faith, some great people I had the good fortune to meet, and some bonds that will stay with me forever. I owe my heartfelt thanks to all those who have been part of this journey, each in their own way, who provided company, comfort, food and jobs when I needed them the most, and helped me push my limits to complete a journey that seemed almost impossible at more than one point.

Thanks to my parents for believing in me and for letting me be me. They have always encouraged me to take the road less travelled—a way unimagined in many middle-class families. I could not have hoped to finish writing this book if I had not been given the time and space to lock myself up in a room to pen down these experiences after being away from home constantly for seven months.

Thanks to some of the greatest friends who have been my biggest cheerleaders and added the right share of fun and adventure to this journey. To some of the greatest minds for transforming ideas into reality and to those who made me who I am today as an individual and as a professional.

I owe special thanks to Ravi Singh, the publisher of

Speaking Tiger Books, for believing in the idea, and Renuka Chatterjee, VP, Publishing, for bearing with my countless emails for clarifications. My heartfelt gratitude and thanks to my editor, Saroja Khanna, for giving this idea a new face.

Many thanks to Akshaya Bahibala, well known as the co-founder of the Walking Book Fair, for never giving up on me—he never lost faith in the idea that this book would hit the bookstores and many like you could be reading it one day.

Lastly, my thanks and heart to my wife Tias for being absolutely cool with no mention of her in the book though she remains one of the most important people I met during this journey—one of my few 'forevers'. She deserves to be celebrated as a partner for letting me republish this book with its fair share of truth and fiction as they were a decade back.

And yes, I want to thank YOU for choosing this book.

Prologue

My hometown is Sonepur, a place in the state of Odisha. We lived in a small village, where my father worked as a teacher in a government school until I was two years old. Before my elder sister and I started our schooling, my father decided to shift to Sonepur, the place where he was born and had been brought up. The primary reason was so that we could get a better education. The shift to Sonepur meant that my father had to cycle some 25-kilometres every day to reach his school, but parents often make sacrifices for their children.

Sonepur is a very old town, where civilization grew at the confluence of two rivers. People called the other side of the river *videsh*, the foreign land. Because of the ghats and hundreds of temples, Sonepur is often called the Varanasi of Odisha. We would include the nearest temple in our postal address as even though there are many temples in the small town, each is distinct as a landmark.

I have watched this place evolve over the years. I remember how my cousins had bunked college and sat on a strike to demand a separate district for Sonepur, and how they celebrated when the demand was granted. I remember I used to go to my neighbour's house to watch the *Ramayana* serial on TV. Sometimes the door opened after several knocks; sometimes it didn't. My father understood his children's desire and brought home a TV. Later, cable television replaced the distinctly monotonous tone of Doordarshan.

When water points were installed in Sonepur, my sister and I were given two tiny buckets to fetch some home. We would race back, seeing who could get home first. People stopped depending on the river for their water supply after that, but I still missed that life. Half of my childhood had been spent on the river Mahanadi, on whose banks we used to fly kites, running over the sand. I was never good at sports but in the water, none of my friends could beat me at swimming.

I recall when the muddy streets transformed into concrete roads. I was against it at the time as I was learning to cycle and knew it would hurt less to fall on a muddy street than concrete.

Rathayatra is the main festival in our home, and I was brought up with the blessings of Lord Jagannath. Carrying the idols to the cart was the most enjoyable part of the Rathayatra. In those days, many of the kids would gather in our home to do that and be part of the celebration. I would argue with my cousins and insist on carrying the bigger idols, which were too heavy for me. By the time I grew old enough to hold the bigger idols and pull the carts, the video game culture had slowly crept into the small town. My friends were no longer interested in our celebrations.

Although brought up in an orthodox Brahmin community, I started questioning many brahminical practices as I grew older. We laughed when a Brahmin showed his *janayu* (sacred thread) to get few more rasagollas than others. Once during my high school days when a family invited me for a Brahman Bhojan, I was not allowed to sit with the old pundits as I had turned up in torn jeans and a casual black T-shirt.

Many changes happened after I received the district topper award for boys from the District Collector. My father decided to send me to the nearest city, Sambalpur, for my intermediate studies. His reasoning was that I would get more competetive with better students there. But actually I was trying to compete with myself and struggling with the switch in the medium of education from Odia to the English language.

During this period, from 1998 to 2000, I experienced two new things: hostel life and English. I became more independent and understood the importance of friendships. As I was struggling to understand the lectures in English, I was forced to spend a lot of time out of the class. What I would study were the routes and paths all the beautiful girls in my classes would take to the nearest crossroad for tuitions.

My mother worried about my ability to pass the intermediate exams. Much to her relief, I managed to get a first division, and I was happy that I didn't have to cross the river again to catch a bus.

Sambalpur is around 80 kilometres away on the other side of the river so I used to take a boat and cross the river, the long and wide Mahanadi, to catch a bus from there. Throughout my intermediate, I hoped the construction of the bridge would be finished, and I could catch the bus from our nearest bus stand. But by the time it was ready, I had already finished with my schooling. Once the bridge was in use, people stopped calling the other side *videsh*. Urbanization had reduced the distance.

Sonepur was part of the undivided KBK districts (Kalahandi–Bolangir–Koraput region), one of the most backward regions in the country, according to the Planning Commission of India. There was a continuous flow of money to the region from the Backward Regions Grant Fund Programme.

At that point in time, we had an average literacy rate of 74 per cent, higher than the national average of 59.5 per cent, with male literacy at 82 per cent, and female literacy at 65 per cent. Still, we were considered backward according to the poverty line measure. In a radius of one kilometre from our house, we had some five FTII graduates, two Padmashree awardees for art and handlooms, one astronomer who had discovered a galaxy, a very reputed environmental journalist, and many other versatile talents. But despite this variety of high performers, when the time came to choose a profession, Sonepur was no different from most other places, where parents thought there were only two streams worthy of education: engineering and medicine.

Medicine was out of the question for me as I had not opted for biology in my intermediate. So the only option was engineering. My father asked me where I wanted to go for my JEE (Joint Entrance Examination) preparation, but I had always wanted to do something in a creative field. However, I was not mature enough to know what that something was, and there was no one in my family to guide me.

That was a time when anyone and everyone who cleared a computer certification course dreamt of going to the USA to work in the software industry. In my huge extended family, the highest educational qualification was held by a cousin who was studying engineering at a private college in Bhubaneswar. We were told that the fat income jobs were in the IT industry, where you could get a monthly salary of 20-25,000 rupees, a big amount for a middle-class boy like me. My sister passed her intermediate exams with a second class and decided not to opt for professional studies. This too added to the pressure on me to choose engineering.

It was as if engineering had chosen me and not the other way round. But the good thing was that engineering turned out to be fun, as I was introduced to the world of computer programming. I made some best friends. I also got involved in various cocurricular activities and excelled at them, which made me overconfident. I remember that I had a crush on my Java teacher. In the first Java lab, I did some complex coding to impress her, instead of the simpler lab assignment. My friends were always there as partners in crime to egg me on. And then the glory days got over, and working life began.

As life moved on, I started believing that each person's life is dominated by one city. For me, that place was Chennai, where I held my first job, as a software engineer, and encountered my first love, Sameen. But in the case of both job and love I quickly realized that I had entered someone else's territory.

When Sameen came into my life, she had already chosen her life partner. Love often strikes where it is forbidden. I knew we could be friends, but nothing more. I had never had these strong feelings for any girl before. I couldn't change the feelings I had for her just because she came into my life when it was too late, or because she was from a different religion.

I remember the first time one of my colleagues introduced us. Her dupatta was wrapped around her face and I noticed she had a radiant, innocent smile. When we started talking, it did not feel as though it was for the first time. Our friendship grew with time, and we often met on the weekends. But each time, I was reminded that my love for her was and would probably always remain unreciprocated. The only time I cried was when I realized that I would be unable to express my suppressed feelings to her. I felt lost and weak when Sameen left Chennai rather suddenly, something I had least expected and was not able to handle emotionally.

I decided to take a week off from work and go home. One afternoon as I was sitting on the verandah, looking at the mango tree and watching a beautiful parrot eat a half-bitten mango, I realized it had been years since I had enjoyed watching such small things. Looking at the garden, I realized a lot of things had changed in the years since I had left home. The banana trees almost reached the well, running wild from lack of tending, and two small mango trees had begun to germinate from the free-falling fruits. The guava tree had reached a height where one could pluck a fruit from the first floor window. The state of the garden was telling me that my parents were getting old.

My thoughts were derailed when my mother came and sat next to me. She handed me a semi-ripe carambola; she knew how much I enjoyed the star fruit. Carambola usually tastes sour, but the tree in our garden produced fruits with a sweeter taste.

My mother loved to tell me stories about our past, and they always fascinated me. She had been brought up along with eight siblings. Her marriage had been fixed with an exchange of coconuts. When she moved to my father's place, they had at first struggled financially and she had faced a lot of drama from her mother-in-law. She would also tell me about her experiences with me and my sister, and the trouble we had given her. While sitting there that afternoon I told her about my dream to travel around India, and she in turn narrated my paternal grandfather's story.

Sonepur was a small kingdom in the colonial era. Circa 1920, a motherless Brahmin child was seen crying in front of a temple here. His father had brought him from the other side of the river to sell him, and then embark on a Chardham Yatra, a pilgrimage to four major religious sites of Hindus: Badrinath, Dwarka, Puri and Rameswaram. Travellers often feared that they might never return, so they usually did their own *shraddh*, one of several last rites, and settled other matters, before heading out on the journey. It so happened that a Brahmin couple were doing a yangya, a ritual, inside the same temple to fulfil their dream of having a child. The couple saw the crying child in front of the temple and they decided to adopt him. That child was my grandfather.

Travel, it seems, was in my genes. My grandfather had travelled to most of the places of religious significance to the family, as had my parents. And now I planned to join their ranks. Travel was on the cards but what I had in mind was not a pilgrimage tour.

'You were the topper in school, right?' my mother asked suddenly. I didn't see how this question had any connection to what we were discussing. 'Are you happy?' she asked. 'Is this what you wanted to be?' This question gave me some idea of where the conversation was likely headed, and I spoke honestly. 'No.' She just smiled.

I was in my mid-twenties by then, working with an IT firm, and earning well. Being from a small town, middle-class family, I thought my parents were happy to boast about me in the neighbourhood. But I was stunned by her thought-provoking question. My mother's world starts at our house and ends three houses to the left and four houses to the right. This is her tiny world and her observations and comments are centred there. She told me that at least one person from every family near our house had become a software engineer. I had never thought about it before, but that was so. The booming privatization of engineering colleges in the last ten years had made the dream of becoming an engineer the easiest one to achieve. What was the point to my being the topper then? Was every Indian child's dream really to become an engineer?

That question kept haunting me: why do most people compromise on their dreams at an early age and choose the stereotypical paths of engineering or medicine? Do we lack in creativity? Does parental interference and societal status force students to choose this path? Why do people fear to follow their passion, to chase their dreams to become what they really wanted to be?

There were a few more incidents that made me think about this again and again. I am a big movie buff, and many movies have made me introspect. I was envious of the protagonist of the film *Slumdog Millionaire*. As the story unfolds, a youngster tries his hand at many things to survive, working as a beggar, selling goods, selling toys on trains, working as a tour guide, a photographer, providing chai to corporate workers, seeing the workings of a BPO. He did not have to think about what society would think about him before taking decisions regarding his next career step. If you don't have anything, there is no fear of losing anything.

Another movie that inspired me a lot was the Aamir Khan starrer, *3 Idiots*. It presented an altogether different approach to choosing a career and a passion. The beautiful message in that movie struck a chord: Don't run behind success. Go behind excellence and success will follow.

Between 2006 and 2009, while working in the IT sector, I realized that I had entered the wrong profession. I had planned to do a master's after my engineering degree, and I was clear that I didn't want to compromise on the subjects of my interest. I wanted to do a master's in HCI, which is a combination of computer engineering, psychology, and design. There were a few universities in the US that offered the course. But here too, the main problem I faced was English. I needed to crack the GRE. The Graduate Record Examinations required mugging up a few thousand words and more. I could not get through it, but the preparation helped me crack other competitive exams and earn a seat at MICA in Ahmedabad, the management institute noted as a school of ideas. Nothing could have been better than that. I had finally found the right track to move forward.

With those questions repeatedly bubbling in my mind, I came up with an idea. I would travel around India and try my hand at a range of professions in different places. This would be a good way to explore a variety of jobs in diverse settings while, hopefully, observing people who were living their passion.

The idea lay dormant for two years, till I turned 28. By that age one has had enough time, circumstances and finances permitting, to get an education, settle into some profession, try all things like alcohol and weed, fall in love, have affairs, realize that love, sex and marriage are three different things, get married, have kids, and take up the responsibility of a family.

But in my case, my heart was still stuck on Sameen. When we are young, we believe there will be many people with whom we will connect, but later we realize that those we miss the most are the special ones. I had heard that Sameen was in Delhi so I moved there. Meanwhile, my parents were worried about my marriage.

When I looked back on life, I saw myself as a winner who had lost his heart to someone he never got, an employee who was still looking for the ideal work culture, a philosopher whose only philosophy was to live a cheap and ridiculous life, a writer who only wrote about someone he had lost but hoped to meet again. I didn't want to have any regrets about not exploring my ideas, but the only thing missing was the trigger to move.

Prologue

It came when my parents wouldn't listen to any of my arguments on delaying my marriage. One day we had a big argument over the phone, and I had to hang up mid-call. They wanted to get me settled, which in India means getting married. I didn't want to regret not living my dreams, so I kept my phone switched off for a month and started working on route plans. When I came across Sean Aiken and his One Week Job Project in Canada it was just the real-life inspiration I needed.

Once the idea of doing different jobs came into my mind, I googled to see if anyone had done something similar. I found Sean Aiken, who had done 52 jobs in 52 weeks in Canada, spreading his message to youngsters to 'Discover Your Passion'. His One Week Job Project had been carried forward in different countries like the US, Australia, the United Kingdom, etc. So I wrote an email to Sean Aiken about my interest in collaborating on the project. That's how the One Week Job project took shape in India. My plan was to do 28 jobs in 28 states instead of Aiken's 52 Jobs in 52 Weeks. Finally, my journey of spending 28 weeks in 28 different states in India, experiencing 28 different work cultures, started to take shape in 2013.

My first step was to plan the route. I didn't have a clue about many of the states, and I had to arrange for jobs through a random approach. The list of rejections grew longer day by day. Some of the experiences I really wanted to explore included working in a gun house in Nagaland, as a zoo caretaker, a light boy in a movie production house, and at a cremation ghat in Varanasi.

After talking to a few friends I created a crowdfunding campaign on a platform called Wishberry, and requested friends and others known to me to support my project. More than the crowdfunding, the most difficult part was convincing employers to hire me for a one-week job. I tried to arrange jobs in advance through phone calls, social media and email, and many through personal contacts. Many of those I contacted were hesitant as they felt offering me a one-week job would not add any value to their organization. Fortunately a few were more open to the idea and agreed to pay a token amount; some suggested a week of voluntary work.

This '28 Jobs' project was a challenge I had set for myself. I was determined to finish it in seven to eight months, keeping in mind some extra time considering the diverse terrain, the possibility of uncertain climatic conditions and, just in case of any health problems.

This was the path I chose to discover my passion. However, I'm not advocating the 28 jobs route to do so. It's more about each individual setting themselves a challenge that suits them—and working hard and with focus to achieve it. While it would be presumptuous to draw a parallel, I do take inspiration from the Buddha who discovered his path to nirvana but never claimed that it was the only path.

The journey I had embarked on, the entire experience, helped me put in perspective the role of passion as a motivator when choosing one's profession.

1. Gujarat

Cheers to Single Malt in a 'Dry State'!

I was very excited. My journey would be starting the next day! I had never travelled for such a long time in one stretch; I had never knocked on random doors asking for shelter, nor had I approached unknown people asking for a job. I was prepared to sleep under the open sky, to try my hand at the most unusual jobs I could come across over the next seven months. I was completely clueless about how it would fall into place. I was excited and scared at the same time. Starting the journey from the state of Gujarat where I did my post graduate studies would, I thought, make me feel less anxious.

I headed for Ahmedabad from Delhi. Many of my friends had offered to put me up in Ahmedabad, so I was not worried about accommodation. Shakti, one of my seniors at MICA, was one of them. He was an avid traveller who had covered many parts of India, and I was excited about discussing and brainstorming my itinerary with him.

Shakti was waiting for me at the bus terminus in Ahmedabad. He took me to a restaurant where we had awesome mutton biryani before heading to his house. His long stay in the city had made him an expert on where to get the best non-vegetarian food in the land of Krishna and Gandhi.

Gujarat is probably the only state in the country where it's not easy to find non-vegetarian dishes even in the major restaurants. Because of the overwhelmingly vegetarian set-up, even the food giant Pizza Hut had opened its first vegetarian pizza outlet here. While we enjoyed our meal, Shakti grilled me on my proposed plan. It was the first time I was discussing my project with someone who had more confidence in it than I myself did. He also gave me a few contacts for jobs in different states. We refrained from planning out the details of my travel as I wanted to leave much of it to chance.

In Ahmedabad, I had an offer to work as a market researcher in Brand Aid Pvt Ltd. The integrated marketing communication firm dealt with industrial corporate branding on different media. I received the offer through my friend Hiral, who called me once she learned of my project. I had tried my best not to take too many jobs from my own friends' circle, but good friends don't like to hear the word 'no'. Hiral knew that entrepreneurship was my passion, and she offered me a job of primary research for a new vertical setup of the signage business in their company. She was the head of the events division in Brand Aid, and recommended my name to the MD.

The office was easy to locate thanks to it being in a well-known locality near the Karnavati Club. Once I reached the office, I was told to wait to meet the HR person. Following a quick introduction to the company, she introduced me to people from different departments: design, branding solutions, events, animation, films, advertising, internet marketing, web solutions and others. This made me realize that instead of going to 28 states for 28 different jobs, one can experience 28 kinds of work in the same organization!

There was a very interesting project going on in the animation section. They were working on a depiction of Mahatma Gandhi's life in pictorial book format as well as through an animated film. Both the book and the film were going to be released in multiple languages. They had completed the ones in English, Hindi and Gujarati. Being an Odia, I told the HR people that if they were looking for an Odia translator, I would love to do the project.

Then I met the managing director, Hiten Shah. Hiten was a very friendly person and had good business sense thanks to his decades' long experience. He called Kaushal, the colleague I would be partnering with for the week, and explained my job. I was to study the signage market, the number of players already in Gujarat, the possibilities of signage type, the total market value of the business, potential clients, pros and cons of handling a government tender, signage opportunities in the Indian Railways and the Airports Authority of India, and finally, the evolving digital signage business. Kaushal explained the kind of signage they had already worked on in their pilot project. Hiten instructed Kaushal to give me more details, as well as to arrange for a desktop.

Having already experienced a few office jobs in the course of my career, I had planned not to repeat them along my journey. I wanted to take up as many field jobs as possible. But office jobs have their own advantages. You need to work smart, rather than hard. If you complete the job before the assigned date, then you could get a lot of free time. You get to enjoy an air-conditioned environment as well as high-speed internet, which gives you access to social networking sites. Intellectually demanding jobs always pay well.

Once I got a computer, I realized that if I had any free time, I would enjoy writing about my experiences alongside work. I opened Facebook to see that my friend Gurvinder had tagged me in a photo, a screenshot from the *Mid-Day* newspaper of that day. More than a hundred of my friends had commented on it, wishing me luck for my journey. One Week Job India had been featured in *Mid-Day Mumbai* on the front page. There could not have been a better start to my journey as it helped get a few more job offers through social media.

Signage refers to the graphic display information for navigational purposes. I had seen it in many places like streets, outside buildings, malls, airports, petrol pumps and so on. After digital signage entered the market, it could be seen in banks, corporate buildings, buses and even grocery stores. I divided my research along four major verticals: education, retail, transport and the government sector. Researching and learning about new topics had always interested me, and I was sure I would enjoy my work for the week.

Hiral greeted me in her characteristic manner: 'Hiiiiiiiiii Juba!' We were meeting after nearly two years. She seemed more mature, bolder and prosperous, and more elegant. She had started her career in events ten years back. Before moving to Ahmedabad from Mumbai, her last big project had been as an executive producer with *Comedy Circus*, among the most popular TV series of that time. Hiral had always loved to plan events. That was her forte and she could work day and night at a stretch during big events. From the outset of my journey I was fortunate to connect with people who lived their passion!

Hiral invited me to join her for lunch. We had delicious paneer kulcha and raita at Bikanerwala, right next to our office. Hiral had spent that morning in a meeting with Gujarat Tourism. She was handling a new event that was to take place in Kutch and enjoying her work. You can recognize passionate people by talking to them; even if they try their best not to talk about their favourite topic, they can't resist roping it into the conversation.

Kutch is known for being one of the largest salt deserts in the world. Popularly known as the Rann of Kutch, it spreads between the Thar Desert in the Kutch District of Gujarat and the Sindh province of Pakistan. I had been there once, during my MICA days, when I spent a night above the salt desert with the moonlight reflecting off the sand.

The Tourism Board was organizing an event called Run the Rann to promote adventure sports and eco-tourism in the state. It was open to runners from across the world. Through this event, Gujarat Tourism was trying to place the state on the global running circuit. Many noted athletes were expected to take part. Sports tourism is still a very nascent scene in India, and Gujarat was breaking new ground with the Run.

At the end of the day, Shakti called me to say he would be picking me up from the office. We would be visiting MICA.

Coming to Ahmedabad and not going to your second home would seem like an incomplete visit.

When I quit my IT job, I had been hoping to enrol for a master's degree in the US. When that didn't work out, there was some trepidation in my heart. The future was so uncertain. Once I had handed over my company ID card to the TCS HR department, I almost felt like a product with no brand value. Even if we are not happy with our jobs, some kind of association with a big company adds brand value. On my way home, I sat down in a graveyard for a while and pondered on my decision. It was there that I got a call from a friend. 'Dude, you got through to MICA, the school of ideas!' he said.

I realized one thing that day—quite often you reach the place you are destined for, even if you never try or wish for it. I had never wanted to do an MBA, had never even prepared for one. My perception of management school changed after I got into one. That was the best thing that had happened to me. It helped shape me in a lot of ways, changing my thought process, teaching me to accept each person as they are. The best thing I learned at MICA was that there is always a grey region between white and black, and we should accept those shades of grey as well.

These memories flashed into my mind as I entered the MICA gate. The head security guard who opened the main gate to the campus knew the names of almost every inhabitant, including old students, teachers and other staff members. He opened the gate with a huge smile. '*Kaka, kaise ho?*' I addressed him as uncle and asked how he was.

I had brought him a packet of one of his favourite snacks. Whenever we used to go out of the campus during our college days, I would return with a special namkeen that he had once told me he liked.

He was always concerned and would say so if we didn't wear helmets while riding bikes. Although it was by then mandatory in Ahmedabad for two-wheeler riders to wear them, our standard reply was that the traffic police weren't strict about the rule.

He was surprised to see me. Very few students were on campus during the summer break except for those there for the summer internship. '*Abhi kahan aya, summer internship chal raha hai?*' I told him that since I was in town for a project, I was keen to visit my old campus. He looked pleased and patted by back.

I have a sentimental weakness for MICA and obviously have lots of nostalgic memories. Among those that came flooding back were of boisterous birthday celebrations, the first monsoon rains, shouting to turn up the volume coming from the next room, a Mandvi beach trip where I was talking to the moon in an intoxicated state, searching for lions in an open safari on a Gir forest trip, the last exam preparation and the final convocation. All those scenes were flashing back in my mind while we walked down from the Silver Oak hostel towards Chotta canteen, our favourite hang-out. It had become larger. I realized even *Chotta* becomes *Badaa* with time.

I didn't want to miss sitting on the truck tyre hanging from the tree. With just a few squirrels there and very few students the campus felt lonely rather than serene. I was missing my friends a lot. When Roxy, our campus dog, approached us it felt less lonely there.

The week flew by very quickly. I enjoyed the friendly office environment, satiated my appetite with delicious Ahmedabad food, and met some good old friends. On the last day, I made a presentation to Hiten, summarizing my work on the signage vertical. Kaushal picked out a few points from the presentation and discussed them with Hiten, trying to figure out the best way to take it forward.

Hiral invited me, Shakti and another colleague, Rahul, to dinner at her place. While showing off her beautiful apartment, she said, 'I have arranged a barbecue, and everyone has to prepare their own food.' I responded foolishly, 'I only know how to cook *desi khana*!'

'Juba, you know that whatever you do, wherever you reach, you will always be a *desi*,' remarked Hiral. I took it in good humour, laughed and thanked her.

We followed her to the terrace. She had arranged all the equipment for the barbecue: a charcoal heater, iron skewers, and a large bowl of marinated vegetables. Shakti sat on the swing and said that the evening was perfect for a drinking session. Hiral was prepared and soon there was a bottle on the table. 'Juba, I have single malt whiskey for you,' she said.

The Gujarat state government has a ban on alcohol, but it is not that difficult to get. I remember how we used to summon Folder, the bootlegger guy, for our college parties. He usually charged thrice the retail price for whiskey. That was a phase when we tasted all the cheap brands we had never tried before. We were not always lucky enough to get single malt whiskey.

On my last evening in Ahmedabad, I visited the popular Natrani amphitheatre. During my college days I had enjoyed short films there, under the open sky and set against the backdrop of the serene river Sabarmati. The screenings and the setting together stoked my interest in the place.

Cyrus Dastur founded Shamiana, at that time India's biggest short films club. Shamiana turned out to be a real inspiration for many short film-makers. My brainchild, the International Short Film Festival Bhubaneswar started in 2011, was inspired by Dastur's club.

When I greeted Cyrus, he was surprised by my unexpected visit. I told him about my project and the documentary film I was planning to make about my journey.

Cyrus liked to introduce every film before the screening. That evening he announced, 'My friend Jubanashwa is travelling around India, doing 28 jobs in 28 weeks in all the 28 states. He is making a documentary film about it. Let's call him to the stage!'

I wasn't sure what to talk about as I had just started the journey. In terms of the documentary, I had just recorded some footage, and was not even sure about the flow of the movie. Cyrus made it easy for me by asking me questions and holding a small discussion on the stage. I was staring at a beautiful girl sitting in the audience. Her face looked familiar, but I couldn't place her. After the screenings, Cyrus welcomed a few young talents, and she was among them.

After Cyrus's introduction, I realized that I had seen her

many times on television. She was Aishwarya Majumdar, winner of Amul's Star Voice of India. Her voice was one of the sweetest I had ever heard. She sang a very popular old Hindi song that night: *Aaj jaane ki zid na karo*. I was leaving for Udaipur the next day, and no song could have been more apt. The more attention I paid to the lyrics, the more I fell in love with it. I would stick by these lines for the next few months, living to the present, looking forward to what lay ahead.

> *Waqt ki qaid mein zindagi hai magar*
> *Chand ghariyaan yehi hain jo aazaad hain*
> *Inko kho kar meri jaan-e-jaan*
> *Umr bhar na taraste raho*
> *Aaj jaane ki zid na karo.*

2. Rajasthan

My First Encounter with World Travellers

Unlike my previous trip, I didn't even bother to book a ticket from Ahmedabad to Udaipur. It was a distance of just 250 kilometres. Shakti reignited my own carefree mindset with his idea that I should experience a road trip to Udaipur by truck. I would reach the city by Sunday night, and start work as a hotel manager from Monday morning.

Early the next morning, we headed to NH 8 to flag down a truck. Finally, after many rejections, one trucker was willing to give me a lift to Udaipur. He was a Sardarji and I spoke few lines in Punjabi to convince him. He told me to get on but only if I wasn't too worried about our time of arrival. I said I was okay with this. He responded with '*Aajaa phir*', come on then. Shakti wished me luck and waved goodbye.

There was another guy on board who helped me with my baggage. He was very curious about the obvious discrepancy between my luggage and my mode of travel. '*Aap toh AC Volvo mein jaa sakte hain, truck mein lift kyon maang rahe the?*' he asked, wanting to know why I was travelling in a truck when I could afford a Volvo bus. I told him that I wanted to experience a truck ride. He was not convinced. The driver was curious and asked, 'Have you ever been in a truck before?' I told him I hadn't.

He had decorated his truck in a very colourful manner. When I complimented him on it he smiled and said 'This is my second wife'. There were many things tied to the back of the truck to ward off 'evil eyes' such as lemon strung with some green chilies, and black tassels. I learned from the other guy that the truck was carrying Honda scooters from Ahmedabad to Udaipur.

By the time we reached Udaipur it was late, well past eleven.

I had looked for a job in a haveli to experience the workings of a heritage mansion but ended up with a mid-range hotel. In response to my request by email, the owner of the hotel had offered me the post of manager.

When I introduced myself to the person on duty at the hotel, he questioned my late arrival. 'You were supposed to reach here by evening,' said Pushpendu, the hotel manager I would report to for the week.

There were hardly any residents at the reception. Pushpendu told me to report at nine in the morning and called a youngster to take me to the staff quarters. The hotel had rented a house for the staff which was about 100 metres from the hotel. A huge hall had been partitioned with plywood. The bigger portion was for the kitchen staff, with two comparatively smaller rooms for room attendants and housekeepers, and two individual rooms for the hotel managers. One of the managers had recently left the job, so I was lucky to get his room. I opened the window and switched on the table fan. After a welcome bath, I slipped into bed and fell asleep.

I had visited Udaipur with my parents two years earlier, and I did recall a few of the popular places: the City Palace, Fateh Sagar Lake, Lake Pichola, and the Jagdish Temple. Travels with my parents always included visits to temples, and I do enjoy the architecture. Tourists from around the globe visit the city, and the hospitality business has kept pace, growing year by year. Its popularity is such that even though it is almost unbearably hot in the summer, tourists can still be spotted.

The next morning, I reported to Pushpendu as scheduled. I had noted his attire of the previous night, so I too wore a white shirt and black trousers. I couldn't remember ever wearing a white shirt except at my convocation. Pushpendu gave me a brief on the hotel, its facilities, departments and the staff. He told me to remember every minute detail so that I could answer queries from new guests.

Each of the twenty rooms on three floors was decorated in the traditional haveli style. Pushpendu walked me through all the floors. The multicuisine restaurant on the top floor adjoined an open-air swimming pool. In the kitchen, he showed me how the kitchen implements needed to be checked and sorted, every day.

He listed the daily housekeeping activities that had to be done for every room. My main job would be to oversee the housekeeping arrangements as well as entertain visitors and answer their queries in the reception area.

We started our housekeeping routine late in the morning, when most of the residents had either checked out or were out sightseeing. Pushpendu gave me a checklist to monitor each of the tasks to be executed, and sent Manish, a room attendant, to accompany me on my first day. Two housekeeping staff would be working alongside, one to clean the room and other to clean the bathroom. I could see the caste system playing out, as it has for centuries.

The first room we entered was very messy. While Manish ran through all the points I had to monitor, the house cleaners started their work of cleaning the room, wiping the mirrors and mopping the floor. The guy seemed to be an expert at making a bed. I observed the systematic way he did it. First, he pulled the mattress a little away from the headboard, and removed the blankets and the soiled bedsheet. Then he spread a clean sheet over the mattress and tucked the corners in very neatly. He tucked the blanket around three sides of the bed and folded it down at the pillow end. After changing the pillow covers he pushed the mattress flush towards the headboard. He folded the towels to resemble the shapes of doves and flowers and placed them on the freshly-made bed.

Manish was quite a funny guy and cracked jokes from time to time. 'We are trying to encourage honeymooning couples to throw their used condoms in the dustbins rather than flushing them down the toilet,' he said but didn't explain how. Instead he said that newly-married couples from small towns in India usually hid the used condoms under the mattress or flushed them down the toilet, almost as though they had committed a crime.

One cleaning boy was busy disinfecting the toilet, toilet seat, bath tub, sink and mirror. He checked for soaps and shampoo bottles that needed to be replaced, changed the towels with fresh ones and emptied the dustbin. Once we were through with all the rooms, we headed for the restaurant.

While cleaning activities in the kitchen were handled by the staff of that department, other cleaners took care of the restaurant. Pushpendu was in the restaurant supervising the cleaning. He told me to go to the reception to attend to the guests.

Manish took me to the terrace and we smoked a *beedi*. I accepted as sharing a smoke often helps create bonds. That could be handy during my week there, I thought. The reception area was spacious with five big sofas, chairs and coffee tables. For most of the day it was used by the staff, chitchatting and watching TV. Mornings were the peak period at the reception, when guests would check out and new ones would check in, and in the evening when residents came back from sightseeing. I was enjoying my job at the reception desk, entertaining visitors' queries, and attending to calls for room service.

I was impressed with Pushpendu's efficiency at managing the staff. Manish was always in a hyperactive state, cracking jokes, making the other staff members laugh and generally making the environment lively.

It was quite amusing to see Manish in action when Pushpendu asked him to show the others how the tourist guides advertised the hotel. He enjoyed emphasizing how the guides exaggerated every tiny thing to make it sound not only very comfortable but also close to places of historical interest.

Manish was quite comical as he acted out the part. 'This is good hotel, very very good hotel. AC rooms available, hot water you need available, cold water bhi available, 24-hour service ... anything you want. Staff are good, very very good. Swimming pool, top floor, restaurant, terrace. Aravali Hills, Gulab Bagh walking distance ... very near... you stay here. I take you City Palace, Lake Palace, Zoo. You want to see traditional dance, I will take you. Meera Kala Mandir, Udaipur is the city of lakes, many lakes, Pichola lake, Fateh Sagar lake. It is Venice of India, you will love it. Many Hollywood films shoot here. Like many lakes many palaces here—Maharana Pratap, he the king moved the capital of Mewar kingdom from Chittorgarh to Udaipur. You want to go to Chittorgarh, I arrange taxi. You know *Octopussy*? *Octopussy*, James Bond movie ... shooting here.'

All his information was correct except that Maharana Pratap bit. It was actually Maharana Udai Singh II who had lost Chittorgarh to the Mughal emperor Akbar and moved his capital to Udaipur. Manish would have continued for another ten minutes or more if Pushpendu hadn't made him stop. All the staff were laughing and enjoying the show.

Late night discussions among the residents were enjoyable. I think it's the best part of working in a hotel: you get to interact with new people every day, and there is an interesting story behind every traveller. Like Pushpendu said, this is the only business where you don't need to go anywhere and yet you can travel all around the world.

Every night brought new discussions with new people. People who came on a family trip didn't seem to spend much time in the hall. When there were older travellers chatting, I could sense that the talk would be thoughtful and stretch over a longer period. The younger crowd's conversations invariably started with questions such as where have you come from, and where you are heading to next. Many of the guests were at their laptops or on their cellphones, accessing our unlimited wifi.

One night, a group of travellers in their mid twenties were relaxing on the couches. I was deadly tired that day but listened in to the discussion in my drowsy state. There was a guy from Canada and another from Switzerland sitting on one of the sofas; they had met in McLeodganj. A beautiful French woman who had just arrived from Nepal was seated near them. A guy from Australia had come in from Varanasi, and a girl from America on a year's tour of India was sitting next to him.

'We've just been to Lahaul-Spiti and a few places in the Kinnaur district of Himachal,' said the guy from Switzerland. 'Did you know that some tribes in the Himalayan region still practice polyandry?'

I immediately grew more attentive. He continued. 'When a woman marries a man there, she marries his brothers as well. Every brother in the family has sexual access to the wife.' Everyone looked up and some nodded.

The American girl responded, 'Lahaul-Spiti! I've heard it's a beautiful place.' The discussion took a different turn and grew lackadaisical afterwards. Suddenly, the Swiss guy interjected with another revelation, 'In the Mahabharata, Draupadi marries the five Pandava brothers.' I was very impressed, thinking that the guy was sharing some mythological background to his chosen topic. Everyone joined the discussion except the French woman, and the initiator asked for her opinion.

'But the Pandava brothers were not biological brothers. Their fathers were different,' she said. 'Yuddhisthira was fathered by Yama, Arjuna by Indra, Bhima by Vayu, the other two, the twins Nakula and Sahadeva, sired by Ashvinikumars. So can we say that not only Draupadi, but her mother-in-law too was polyandrous?'

I was stunned by her response.

After some time, the conversation became more general. The Swiss guy shared that he and the Canadian guy were in a relationship. The Australian guy asked if it was love at first sight in McLeodganj.

While I was tuned in to the conversation, I received a call for room service. The woman at the other end asked for an inflatable tube for the swimming pool. I was curious about who wanted to go swimming that late at night so instead of sending an attendant, I went to the pool.

It was the same French woman who had almost brought the conversation to a halt some time earlier. She asked whether I could arrange for a glass of wine. The bar was already closed, but I was not going to say no to a beautiful French woman. I asked Manish for help, and he arranged for it. While decanting the wine I asked, 'So you didn't like the conversation on polyandry?'

'No way,' she said, 'I can't even handle one husband.'

The swimming pool looked bluer in the moonlight, with a clear reflection of the sky. I felt like I was serving wine to a beautiful mermaid floating over the water. We chatted for a while. She revealed that she had married very early. The marriage was over in less than two years. She had wanted to travel around India and do more research on Himalayan studies, and now she was free to chase her dream. She asked me, 'So you were following the conversation in the hall?' I nodded. During her travels over the last few years, she found more solace in reading than in conversations.

World travel can either leave you lonely and dejected, or it can give you new friends with different perspectives on life, perspectives that can make you grow and change as a person. I asked her again, 'So you didn't find today's talk interesting?' Her short reply was 'Been there, seen that.' She added that most in the group would remember the details of the conversation so that they could repeat the same story at their next destination. We both agreed that older people had learned the beauty of conversation—the art of listening and telling good stories.

I had to cut short our chat as Pushpendu had called me to the reception. I wish I could have continued talking to her, but I was on the job. When I got to the reception, I checked her name in the guest register. It was Celine.

*

I was busy at the hotel throughout the week so there was no time to meet any of my friends in Udaipur. Koustubh, a classmate from MICA and a good friend, picked me up on the evening of my last working day. He had started his own venture on branding and communication.

Koustubh took me to a good south Indian restaurant and then to Fateh Sagar. The last time I had been there it was noon. The same landscape looked so different at night. I enjoyed seeing the reflection of the moon on the lake, and the shimmering, glistening water. We parked the car and went for a walk along the east bank.

'I guess you already know about the basic tourist spots in Udaipur,' Koustubh remarked. When I nodded, he added 'Do they play the theme from *Octopussy* every evening in your hotel?' We laughed and he explained that most hotels in the city did that to highlight the fact that the movie had been shot in Udaipur.

He pointed towards the solar observatory set on an island in Fateh Sagar. While we strolled along the bank and ate peanuts, I asked Koustubh about the significance of the colourful burqa worn by a Muslim woman who had just passed by. It was an arida, a distinctive form of burqa, colourful and decorated with patterns and lace, worn by women of the Dawoodi Bohra Muslim community.

Koustubh got a call from home and we headed there. His father had moved from Kolkata to Udaipur, where he had started his career as an electrical engineer.

Koustubh had told his parents about my project. It was the first time I was meeting a friend's parents since I began my journey. I had not told anyone in my family about my journey, except for my sister. I had only told them that I would be travelling across India on some project. I was not sure how Koustubh's parents would react.

To my great joy, they took it very positively. At the dinner table, we discussed many things about my family. Two neighbouring states West Bengal and Odisha were relishing the mutton curry; Brahmins from both the states proud of their non-vegetarian food customs.

During the conversation, I realized that Koustubh's father was unsure of his own son's entrepreneurial journey. My experience had been similar too; I knew the mentality of a middle-class family. I had had to face similar doubts from my parents. Even though I hadn't told them the whole story of doing 28 jobs in as many weeks, they were wary about the idea of travelling across India.

Whenever parents asked me about my unconventional path, I didn't get discouraged or get upset with them as I knew it came from genuine concern. I had proved my parents wrong many times by achieving what I had set out to do. And it was the same for every struggling entrepreneur like Koustubh.

If you are from a middle-class family in India and you want to be the subject of gossip among relatives and neighbours, take an unconventional path. You will be famous in no time. According to the middle-class way of thinking, completing your education at the right time, getting a good job with a good salary and then getting married is what it takes to be settled. Parents are always over-protective and concerned about social status, marriage and financial security. Anyone who follows the path less travelled is looked upon with suspicion. I was no exception.

Koustubh's father asked me how my parents had reacted to my decision to undertake this crazy project. I told him the truth: that I had not told my parents the whole story yet.

My parents were travelling to Badrinath and I hoped to meet them in Delhi on my way to Himachal Pradesh.

3. Himachal Pradesh

Cleaning Hillsides with the Waste Warriors

My parents were on a pilgrimage tour along with some family members, friends and others from our hometown. They had already visited Dwarka, Puri and Rameswaram on earlier tours, and this time would be heading to Badrinath.

I had the details of their itinerary and reached the New Delhi Railway Station well before the train rolled in. This would be a surprise as they were not expecting me. The last time I had spoken to them was from Udaipur.

I spotted my mother getting down, waiting on the platform as my father went back into the train to retrieve the luggage. I patted her on the shoulder, intending to surprise her. She turned around, startled, and scolded me for giving her such a fright in a new place. The next moment however she was all smiles and more than happy to see me.

It was the first time my parents and their pilgrimage group were experiencing the hot, humid climate of Delhi. I filled their water bottles at the nearest water point. All of them were in their mid-50s or older. I stayed with them until their next train left the station, and then made my way to the bus terminal, where I would be boarding the bus to McLeodganj, my next destination.

The guy sitting next to me looked like he had not had a bath for a long time. He had long hair and a dishevelled beard. After some time we started talking, and I learned about his crazy exploration of the civilization on the banks of the river Ganga. Apparently he never planned his travel, giving himself lots of time to explore each place, to collect stories, and gain knowledge. He introduced himself as Samarth from Chennai. Samarth's sarcastic comment on young travellers was, 'I don't qualify for the Yo-traveler tag, because neither do I have an Enfield Bullet nor do I have a DSLR camera.' I laughed when I heard this.

Samarth had started his journey in Gangasagar, where the Ganga empties into the Bay of Bengal. He moved up from here and explored the cities on the banks of the Ganga: Kolkata, Patna, Varanasi, Allahabad, Haridwar, and Rishikesh. He was aiming to reach Gangotri, the origin of the Ganga, after which he planned to go back to Varanasi for a longer period.

I had always been fascinated by Varanasi myself, though I had never been there. I told Samarth about my interest in working as a cremation assistant in Varanasi; that maybe through this One Week One Job India project I would be able to fulfill my dream. We had such a long conversation that I didn't even realize the time until the bus stopped at McLeodganj.

Samarth and I started walking towards Bhagsunag, the place where my office was, and where he too was headed to stay at a yoga retreat. It was less than two kilometres from the bus stop. I was singing *Kadam kadam badaye ja* while plodding ahead with my heavy luggage. Later I came to know that the famous patriotic song had been composed by a Gurkha from this very land.

On the way, I couldn't resist taking out my camera to capture some of the beautiful vistas we saw of the forest and the hills. Once we reached the main square of Bhagsu, Samarth left me and headed towards Dharamkot, about one kilometre from that point. I hoped I would meet him again at some point during my travels.

It wasn't difficult to find the Waste Warriors office, which was just a five-minute walk from Bhagsu square. I would be there for a week, joining a group who were passionate about cleaning up the filth in the region.

The accommodation could not have been better. My lodgings were at the foot of the Himalayas. If you opened the window in the back wall, you could see that the house was built by cutting into some part of the mountain. It was the office-cum-residence of Jodie Underhill, the founder of Waste Warriors, and also lodged a few volunteers.

I had read up on Jodie when one of my friends suggested that I should work in this organization for a week. Jodie is a real inspiration. She had come to India in 2008 as a tourist and had fallen in love with the Himalayas, but the heaps of strewn garbage in Dharamshala bothered her. She decided to help clean up the locality and eventually set up Waste Warriors.

Jodie introduced me to Tashi and Abhi, both senior volunteers who managed the major projects and had been associated with the organization for a long time. Abhi helped me settle down, and briefed me on the basic operations of the organization.

The volunteers went door to door every day on a waste collection drive in the area surrounding Bhagsunag. They then ensured that the waste was disposed of properly. Dustbins, placed in major tourist areas and along the trails of the small town of Bhagsu, were emptied by the workers on a daily basis. A weekly cleaning drive was done in popular tourist hotspots like the Guna Mata temple, Bhagsunag waterfall, and the Triund hill paths. More than ten workers were working on waste collection in different areas.

On my first day I accompanied Pappu, one of the oldest and most experienced of the waste workers. He was from Uttar Pradesh, and had moved to Dharamshala long ago in the hopes of getting a job. Tashi told me to put on a Waste Warrior T-shirt. I wore a pair of gloves, picked up a garbage bag and joined Pappu. We covered business offices, home stays, hotels and households in the nearby area. I noticed that the people were very cooperative and had joined hands with the mission of this organization. Waste collection got over around noon.

In the evening, as I was roaming around Bhagsu, there were moments when I thought I had actually stepped out of India without a visa! The two tiny villages, Dharamkot and Bhagsu, were very popular among Israeli backpackers. Thousands of Israelis came to India each year, looking for peace and spirituality after their year of army service. Many enrolled in meditation courses, yoga, Ayurvedic healing and spiritual practices. Some tried to drown their pain in charas, or grass. Shopkeepers and restaurant owners could speak broken Hebrew, thanks to years of serving them. Many clocks in the phone booths and internet cafés displayed the time in Tel Aviv. Some Israelis who had come here ten years ago had settled down in these villages.

I spent some time in Om Café on the trail to Dharamkot. It was one of the most famous hang-outs in the area. The most frequently used word I heard here was shalom, which can be used to say hello or goodbye in Hebrew. Even the menu was written both in English and Hebrew, and had dishes like hummus and Israeli salad.

Every Tuesday, there was a weekly waste collection session at Triund hill, a famous trekking destination. This time, I accompanied Jodie. She suggested that I carry something warm to wear for when we reached the hilltop. Since I hadn't carried a jacket, I borrowed one from an Irish filmmaker who was lodging with us.

The beauty of the landscape was so absorbing that when we started the journey uphill, I had almost forgotten that I was here to pick up garbage and not to trek. I came crashing back to the real world when I was given a pair of gloves, a litter picker and a garbage bag. We started our journey at noon. Jodie's pet dog Toes came along with us.

We started climbing the mountain right behind our office building instead of walking on the main trail to Triund. We hadn't gone far before we found a trash-filled gully behind a guest house. Jodie tried to convince the manager that we did a daily waste run at every building, and told him not to throw the trash outside the dustbins.

I had gone trekking so many times, but this was the first time I realized the other side of it. I had never thought about what happened to those used water and beverage bottles, coffee cups and chips packets that we so casually chuck anywhere. While continuing our journey, Jodie remarked, 'Rich people have enough money, but they are not concerned about nature.'

We stopped at a tea shop near the Galu Devta temple at the top of Dharamkot, where we separated the waste collected. The trash at the tea stall had already been segregated as the shop owner was very aware and often instructed tourists to drop the waste accordingly. We didn't have to spend much time there and so got on to the main trail which snakes up to Triund. Jodie informed me that there were two more teashops on the way where Waste Warrior dustbins had been installed. The mules that took supplies up to these shops brought the segregated garbage to the main centre.

We spent some time at Magic View Café from where one can enjoy breathtaking views of the entire Kangra valley, Bhagsu, McLeodganj and Dharamshala. From their conversation, I gathered that the guy who ran the place knew Jodie very well. He rolled us a nice joint to help blow away our fatigue after the climb. He was blabbering about the famous varieties of cannabis found across north India: Jammu Chalia, Himachal Charas, Varanasi Ganja.

Most of the people who go to Triund stop for some time at the Magic View Café. This led to a large amount of waste nearby. It took us more than an hour to segregate all the recyclable, non-recyclable, hard plastic and paper waste.

Given the steepness of the trail from there, it was a risky job picking up litter from the ridge and it also demanded a lot of energy. By the time we reached the top, the garbage bags which we had taken from our base point were filled to the brim with chocolate wrappers, bottles, plastic and paper waste. I was totally exhausted, but for Jodie this was nothing new. Luckily the view from the top took my breath away and washed away my tiredness.

There were a number of Israeli backpackers camping on the top of the hill. At that time there was only one guest house at Triund, and it had a very limited number of rooms. We had to share a room with some teenage trekkers we met on the climb. They offered us some puffs of their chillum.

It was really cold at the top of the hill, and the jacket I had borrowed from the Irish filmmaker really saved my life. Thank god we had enough sleeping bags in the guest house, even one for the lovely Toes. I had only carried 300 rupees for the day, which I expected would cover food and refreshment for two days. But up there, food was extremely costly. After dinner, I had only 100 rupees left in my pocket.

Camp fires are the only source of light in Triund. We sat around a camp fire and chatted with travellers from many parts of the world till midnight. I went for a walk, looking up at the beautiful sky, the glittering stars, and campfires from the adjacent knoll. I kept walking till I could no longer hear the sounds of the other travellers.

My birthday was the next day. I had never celebrated my birthday, except on a few occasions in the hostel. It's very strange, sometimes you are in a crowd of a thousand people and you feel alone, and sometimes you are alone at an altitude of over 3000 metres with no electric power or mobile network yet you don't feel lonely. As I walked around on my own, I felt composed and thoughtful.

The next morning, I woke up with a fever and felt quite dizzy, probably due to the constant changes in climate over the last month. I wanted to sleep off the soreness in my muscles, but I had a busy day ahead. We were supposed to collect garbage from all the shops on the hill, segregate it and then climb down to Bhagsu by evening. I got out of bed, determined to complete my task.

First, we collected the garbage from the shops and brought it all to one location. At the two knolls adjacent to Triund, the bulk of the waste we found was alcohol bottles. All the waste we collected was piled into a metre-high mound. Except for biodegradable waste, the Waste Warriors tried to send everything for recycling.

We separated the paper, plastic, glass, and aluminium waste into different containers. I got confused sometimes between the hard plastic and soft plastic. Jodie, who was very fastidious about her work, was irritated by my repeated mistakes. I found her accent hard to follow so I had to listen carefully to catch all her words.

I had more to learn about the segregation process. Tourists often discarded beverage bottles and other containers that still had some of the contents so those had to be emptied before sending them for recycling. There were many containers with remains of curd. I poured these over a rock and crows gathered around.

By the time we had completed our task it was four in the afternoon. It had started raining so we waited for an hour before we started walking down. The tea shop seemed to be doing great business. My mild fever combined with the rain called for a cup of tea.

As soon as the rain stopped we headed back from Triund. Climbing down is more strenuous than climbing up in the mountains. Because of the rains, the path had turned to mush and we had to be very cautious. I stepped on a slippery rock and sprained my ankle. Jodie was far ahead of me by that time. Just as I took a break to loosen up my muscles I saw Toes running towards me. The energy and enthusiasm of the dog pushed me to go on. I was determined not to stop no matter what.

Janessa, a Canadian traveller, was walking behind me, and we started talking. But the pain in my ankle was unbearable so I asked if she wouldn't mind walking slowly so that I could keep up. I told her about my waste collection job, and she noted my Waste Warriors T-shirt. She complimented me on the job, and said she remembered seeing me at the teashop. She told me she was planning to stay in India until her visa expired. Varanasi and the open culture of Goa had really fascinated her. Her only complaint was that there seemed to be more Israelis than Indians in this region!

Jodie was waiting for me when we reached the teashop next to the Galu Devta temple. The sun had set and the only source of light was my cellphone which I had kept switched off due to being out of network coverage. It was a half-hour walk to reach Bhagsu, so we resumed our journey. Jodie had my cellphone torch on to navigate the route. I could see the village lights in the distance, and assumed that we had almost reached when Jodie suddenly declared that we had lost the path. Finally, a villager from Dharamkot helped us to find the way. We sat down in the first bakery we found in Bhagsu. It was already nine at night. Jodie and I were laughing and Janessa joined in.

'So how was the day?' Jodie asked. I said that it was my birthday but added that I wasn't carrying any money so I couldn't give them a treat. Jodie smiled and ordered a Bhagsu cake, which she said was very popular in the area.

When I got into bed that night, it felt like heaven. All the pending messages flooded into my phone and I got many calls as well.

Jodie and Tashi left for the Dehradun Waste Warriors office the next day. They had locked Toes in my room so that he wouldn't rush after them towards the bus stop.

At sunset, I sat on the verandah, looking at the sun playing hide and seek between the trees and reflecting on my time here. Nature fulfils all our basic needs; it's time to think of how we can protect it in return.

I have great respect for Jodie Underhill, who strives to protect nature. She is a woman who is even more concerned about the cleanliness of this area than the local people are. Every revolution starts with a highly dedicated person who believes in the possibility of bringing about change in a small part of the world. I hope her dream can extend throughout India and encourage people to become more concerned about nature.

It was my last day there. Abhi and I went to the Bhagsu waterfall late in the afternoon. The waterfall is one of the most popular destinations in the area and as a result, it gets very dirty. Basically our job was to thoroughly clean the path and retrieve the garbage that had been thrown over the ridge. We held on to the iron railing along the trail to the waterfall and tried to reach the waste using the litter picker. Abhi was a sure-footed climber, leaning out over the edge to collect as much litter as possible. Working with him showed me the more adventurous side to the job.

Right above the falls there are stone steps leading to the Shiva Café. As we walked down the steps, we heard a woman scream 'Snake!' We rushed towards the entrance of the café to check it out. From her long curly hair, I could tell that it was Janessa. In front of her was a snake, its hood raised! Abhi and I were just behind it.

To lighten the mood, I tried to crack a joke. 'Is this cobra trying to impress you by displaying its beautiful hood, or did you frighten it with your scream?' Janessa shouted 'Just shut up!'

Abhi instructed me to empty my garbage bag as quickly as possible. He snatched my litter picker from my hand, and tested the grip. Abhi told Janessa to keep quiet for a moment so that he could distract the snake with the help of the litter picker. As soon as the snake lowered its hood and started moving in its serpentine fashion, Abhi gripped its head with the help of the litter picker. The next moment, he held the head properly so that it could not bite or hurt anyone. He put the snake in the empty bag and closed it tight.

Janessa still looked a little frightened. She was obviously scared of reptiles, like most people are. She asked me to drop her off at her place in Dharamkot.

Janessa had rented a room from a Gaddi family. It was a small room but quite beautiful. 'The smaller the house the larger the happiness,' she said as we walked in. Right next to the room was a terrace with a great view of the mountains.

Janessa looked more relaxed than she had been earlier. 'I think I need a drink,' she said and poured wine into two glasses. Before the glass touched my lips, Janessa had drunk hers in one go and poured herself another. There was a gas stove, and in the middle of the room a few colourful ropes were hanging from the ceiling. They looked quite mysterious and I was curious to know why they were there.

When I asked her about them, she hung herself upside down from those ropes and showed me her yoga practice. She gripped them between her crossed legs, her head touching the ground. She was wearing a loose kurti that slipped down, exposing her round beautiful breasts. I felt a twitch in my pants. In that upside down pose, her head was covered by the kurti and she would not have been able to see anything. It was terrifying to see her in that hanging pose, and yet, she looked beautiful.

When she was back on the ground, her kurti was still in an untidy state and one breast was still partially visible. I stepped out to the terrace. She joined me, holding a bottle of wine in her hand. She offered me the bottle and I accepted it, taking a sip. I realized that she was already drunk, so I placed the bottle out of her reach. Suddenly she asked, 'Why do Indians consider sex as something that should be furtive?'

I didn't have an answer to that. Her blue eyes stared into mine. 'Don't tell me that my breasts didn't turn you on.' She untied her long curly hair and let it fall over her shoulder. We were so close that I felt the warmth of her breath. I turned to look at her, the deep blue lake in her eyes forming a ripple in my heart. She tilted her face and we came closer and kissed momentarily. She slipped her kurti off.

We sat down on the mat on the terrace and kissed passionately. A thought crossed my mind and I looked away from her for a moment. She growled at me, 'What's the matter with you? Are you in love with someone?' I thought it would be better not to answer.

She whispered in my ear as she kissed me. 'The filth is in our minds, not only in our surroundings. Sexual desire is sacred as well as chaste; repressing it takes you away from your own soul.'

4. Punjab

Seva and Langar at the Golden Temple

I was supposed to go to Jammu & Kashmir for my next adventure job as rafting trainee, but after the strenuous mountain cleaning job in Himachal Pradesh, my body told me not to go for it. Instead I was on a bus to Amritsar to visit the Golden Temple and spend a week there in *seva*. In the strictest sense *seva* is not a job, it is selfless service done in all gurudwaras.

Sri Harmandir Sahib, popularly known as the Golden Temple, taught me the beauty of forgiveness. My mind was freed as soon as I touched my forehead to the ground at the gurudwara and looked at the glittering rays coming from the temple. I forgave Sameen, with whom I had tasted the fragrance of love and learned that not everyone is lucky enough to live with their love. It was not my fault that by the time I met her, she was already engaged. I understood that my orthodox father could not have accepted a girl from another religion as a daughter-in-law. My anger at being unlucky in love dissipated. It had taken me five years to open my heart to the beautiful world again, to accept reality. This holy shrine helped to do that, and to clear my mind.

The Golden Temple has four entrances, one in each of the four directions, welcoming people from every corner of the world. I entered through the Chowk Ghanta Ghar side. I was keen to observe the activities going on in the temple as I wanted to spend a week doing *karseva*. *Karseva* or *seva* refers to the selfless service done by Sikhs in all gurudwaras. All Sikhs are encouraged to perform *seva* according to the Guru Granth Sahib, the scripture of Sikhism.

I left my footwear at the shoe counter and proceeded along with the usual crush of visitors towards the entrance. I washed my feet in the small pool of water and took a saffron kerchief from a bucket at the entrance. Covering the head is a sign of respect in Sikhism, and must be done before entering the gurudwara. I heard a Sikh gentleman murmur '*Waheguru Ji Ka Khalsa, Waheguru Ji Ki Fateh*' which means that the Khalsa belongs to the wondrous teacher; the victory belongs to the wondrous teacher. Here Waheguru refers to Guru Nanak, the founder of Sikhism.

One cannot get a glimpse of the Golden Temple from the outside as it is at a lower level than the main road level. I climbed down the steps to reach the sprawling grounds of the temple. Nothing could have been better than seeing the Golden Temple at sunset. The temple is surrounded by a large water pool, a sarovar, and looks as though it is floating on water.

I prostrated myself on the ground as soon as I looked at the temple, a vision that is sacred and serene. The pool is believed to have divine healing powers; many devotees take a holy dip in the sarovar before going for *darshan* or viewing of the sacred.

The sound of Gurbani chants from within gives more energy to the surroundings. I walked all around to get a view of the gorgeous temple. The landscape was vibrant with vivid colours and head coverings: the amazing turbans worn by Sikh men, the colourful clothes worn by women, the dark blue uniforms of temple guardians, the exotic outfits of Sikh holy men, and keski, the small turban worn by young boys.

It was a Sunday evening and there was a very long queue at the entry point. It was nearly an hour before I got a chance to bow down before the Adi Granth Sahib. The holy book is covered with shawls given by its devotees.

The incredibly intricate detailing and gilding on the room's walls and ceiling are beautiful. Given the heavy crowd, it was not possible to spend much time there. After coming out, I went to the drinking water distribution section. There are four drinking water sections, one at each corner of the rectangular temple. There are always a number of volunteers serving water. In the June heat of Amritsar, quenching my thirst with cold water made me feel whole again. My mother always says that there is no way to earn more blessings than by providing water to a thirsty person. For this reason, I wanted to work in the drinking water section.

Before approaching anyone on how to go about volunteering, I walked around to explore more of the temple. Langar halls are designed for people to sit on the floor together and all are served the same food. It symbolizes the equality that prevails over all, from high to low, from rich to poor, from male to female, from Indians to foreigners. Langar, the free kitchen, serves food twice a day to around

50,000 devotees. In the kitchens, the preparation, cooking and washing-up are done by volunteers. Every process is done in a very systematic fashion inside the Langar hall, starting from the distribution of the trays and spoons, guiding each person to a place to sit, and serving dishes at a lightning pace. Within fifteen minutes I had come out of the Langar hall with a full stomach.

Next to the exit point, there was a big space where the dishes were being washed. I watched, fascinated, at how quickly people were working here. I had never seen a better example of the beauty of selfless service. I wanted to start working there right away and set about looking for someone who could provide me more information on the volunteering process.

A man bumped into me, accidentally, as I was heading towards the sarovar. He was rushing towards the Langar hall and asked, '*Kheer mil raha hai kya*? ' 'Yes, I had kheer,' I said. I asked if he was a volunteer. When he said that he served at the drinking water station, I told him that I wanted to serve for a week. He was very happy to hear that and offered to guide me. Anyone can volunteer at gurudwaras but I was happy to have help on how to go about it.

Sarabjeet was studying at a college in Chandigarh. He was from Amritsar and had come home for the summer vacation. He said he usually dedicated his evenings to *karseva*. He took me to the Baba Deep Singh water distribution area and introduced me to another volunteer. That was how I got an opportunity to volunteer for the cleaning section as well. When I thanked Sarabjeet his response was, 'I have not done anything, *sab Guru ki Kripa hai*.'

It was already nine at night by the time I started working. In the first few minutes I realized everything was extremely well organized. The volunteers were focused on listening to the hymns so there was little conversation. The used utensils were being cleaned with wood ash, and most of the volunteers were women. We passed the clean bowls to other volunteers who filled them with water and placed them on a huge marble table for visitors. I tried to work as quickly as Sarabjeet. He checked the first few bowls I had washed.

Sarabjeet told me that the temple receives around 100,000 visitors on normal weekdays, and up to 400,000 during festivals. There were approximately twenty volunteers working at that point of time just at the water unit. He added that there was a lull between nine at night to six in the morning; the rush would grow during the day and become heaviest during the evening. Before he left for home, Sarabjeet said that he usually came in at five in the evening and stayed till ten at night, and that I could find him in the same drinking water section.

The person who replaced Sarabjeet at the cleaning section told me about the governing body of the temple, the Shiromani Gurudwara Parbandhak Committee. The SGPC is the body which is responsible for the upkeep of gurudwaras. The volunteers do service out of devotion and no one dictates their schedules. There is no specific routine for their duties. Everyone comes of their own will and keeps their own schedules. I wondered what would happen if a corporate organization were to give their employees such liberties!

From the next day, I went in for *seva* around noon and stayed till nine at night. I utilized my mornings to write about the jobs and places I had covered till then. I was already in the fourth week of my journey, and had hardly had time to pen the incidents and memories before this.

On my second day I spent some time in an internet café before heading to the temple. When I reached the drinking water point, I didn't recognize any of the volunteers. They were a completely new set of people! I joined them and began washing the bowls.

I still couldn't understand how so many people could work together without any controlling force. When I mentioned this to an elderly volunteer all he said was 'It's just His grace'. It turned out he was a gold merchant and ever since he had started coming here for *seva*, he said his business had grown. He added that one of the tenets of Sikhism is selfless service.

The flow of visitors and volunteers, as Sarabjeet had said, increased towards six in the evening. More than fifty people were serving water at our junction. Volunteers were passing bowls of water to the visitors approaching, rather than waiting for them to reach the marble table, which made the whole process much smoother and faster.

There were more volunteers needed at the wood ash section, so Sarabjeet, who had shown up by then, called me to join him there. He gave me a wide smile and asked whether I was enjoying myself. His point was that people who have noble thoughts always enjoy the goal, and not necessarily the process, but those who enjoy the process feel the divinity.

A woman who was part of our group overheard and she too was all smiles. As we chatted for a bit, I discovered she was a company director who spent her evenings doing *seva*. She said it was an inseparable part of her daily routine.

It was a real eye-opener for me when she pointed out that the drinking water system was eco-friendly. I hadn't even thought about it. It was both efficient and environment-friendly with water distributed to a large number of pilgrims in metal bowls that were rewashed. There were no plastic bottles in sight, and no detergent used, just bio-safe wood ash. In her eight years at the temple she had taken note of this and more.

On festivals and other special occasions in the summer, the temple would serve a mixture of sweetened water and milk. The system was so efficient that it took less than ten minutes to serve the milk from a 300-litre tub!

My week of *seva* was special. It brought tranquility and serenity to the mind. It was amazing to see how the volunteers were so quick to adapt and move from one task and section to another to cater the occasion and the size of the crowd. The part I enjoyed most was serving water, in particular how young children's faces lit up.

A day or two later I saw a young girl bump into Sarabjeet as he was carrying bowls to the cleaning section. The water in her bowl spilled on Sarabjeet's trousers. She apologized quickly and left but oddly, Sarabjeet was all smiles. The same scene was repeated over three consecutive days. In that one week Sarabjeet and I had struck up a friendship so I felt free to ask him what the matter was. He pursed his lips and looked embarrassed. 'I don't know who she is, but she comes in at the same time every day.'

This was a period when I didn't feel like sleeping. Once I was done with *seva* and a meal at the Langar, I would sit near the sarovar and gaze at the beautiful Golden Temple for hours, listening to the kirtan. On some nights, I just put my hands under my head and lay there on the marble floor.

The cleaning routine began at one thirty in the morning. Volunteers would fill buckets at the sarovar and splash it over the marble floors, washing it down and mopping. All the rugs, flowers, the palki, and brass railings were brought out from the interiors to be cleaned. For about an hour, there would be no kirtans.

Late one night, I was sitting on the marble floor, looking at the breathtaking reflection of Harmandir Sahib in the water when a man who appeared to be in his early sixties came and sat next to me. He was looking at the Akal Takht building.

'It was almost destroyed,' he murmured. I could figure out what he was referring to but asked politely, 'Do you mean Operation Blue Star?'

Jarnail Singh Bhindranwale, a militant, had used the Golden Temple to store weapons and create communal tension in Punjab through violent activities. In early June 1984, Prime Minister Indira Gandhi had sanctioned an army operation to remove Bhindranwale and his armed followers from the complex of Harmandir Sahib. Thousands of lives were lost and many people were injured inside this holy complex during the operation. That was what the media reported. It was much later, when I was an adult, that I was able to understand the political complexity of the event.

The man nodded in response to my question and turned his face towards the main temple. After a short silence he asked me whether I was enjoying my visit to Amritsar and the Golden Temple. I told him about my week of doing *seva*. He spoke about how in our traditional Indian society and caste system, work involving physical labour was considered low and relegated to the lowest castes, and *seva*, in the sense of worshipping God, was dominated by the higher castes. Guru Nanak and other Sikh Gurus established the dignity of labour as an honourable religious practice by removing the gap between the castes.

He pointed towards the Akal Takht building. 'It was totally destroyed during Operation Blue Star by the Indian Army.' According to him, Operation Blue Star could have been handled by the civil authorities instead of the military forces. In fact, action should have been taken earlier, when the police could have handled it, right when everyone knew Bhindranwale had moved into temple complex with a hundred armed followers.

I was curious about his interest in the event and asked him what he did. He revealed that he was an ex-serviceman who had quit military service after Operation Blue Star. He said that many Sikh army personnel had left their jobs after Operation Blue Star.

Now I was more conscious as well as curious to learn what he thought of Bhindranwale and Indira Gandhi. I knew that Bhindranwale was considered a saint among those Sikhs who supported the separatist Khalistan movement.

He said that it was Indira Gandhi and the Congress's idea

to set up Bhindranwale with a view to destroying the Akali Dal and creating a rift between Hindus and Sikhs so that they could get all the Hindu votes for their own party. In 1980, after Indira Gandhi's return to power, Bhindranwale used the central government's protection of his increasingly militant activities to great effect. He set himself up as a militant Sikh leader who was capable of defying the government. Even the Akali Dal political party joined hands with the charismatic Bhindranwale. During the next general election, Indira Gandhi was concerned that she would appear weak and indecisive if she failed to act against Bhindranwale. And that opened the doors to Operation Blue Star.

The old man seemed to have a very clear picture of the events. When I asked him why he quit service, he clarified that religion is a personal matter and is respected highly in the military. He criticized the Army for burning down the Sikh Reference Library, which he saw as an attempt to destroy the culture of the Sikhs. 'I was deeply affected,' he said.

*

On my last afternoon in Amritsar, I headed to the Wagah border, a distance of 30 kilometres, in an auto rickshaw. There was a mad rush of spectators gathered to cheer the daily evening Beating Retreat closing ceremony by soldiers of both the nations at the Wagah-Attari border. I found myself a place to sit.

A jawan shouted *'Bharat mata ki...'* and many in the crowd yelled back *'Jai!'* An officer gave some children the Indian flag and they ran with it to the gates of the border.

Patriotic Bollywood tunes blared from loudspeakers and people danced. The Indian and Pakistani soldiers marched up to the gate, acknowledged each other with a salute, and marched back, their knees lifted high up. The display of bravado boosted the crowd's enthusiasm. After sunset, the flags of both countries were lowered and with a firm handshake between the soldiers, the border gates were slammed shut.

5. Jammu & Kashmir

The Waters that Almost Swept Me to Pakistan

My next destination was Reasi district in Jammu & Kashmir, where I had been able to arrange a job as a rafting trainee in an adventure club. I had been to J&K in 2012 with a few friends. Our destination was Leh, Ladakh. We didn't stop at Jammu and instead drove to Leh via Srinagar, Kargil, and a place where our van broke down in middle of nowhere. I had explored a bit of Srinagar and Leh, but Jammu would be a new experience. I took a local bus from the Amritsar interstate bus terminal and headed towards Katra. From there Reasi is 30 kilometres by road. Katra is the place where pilgrims start climbing the hill to Vaishno Devi.

There were a lot of vacant seats, and no one was standing when bus left from Amritsar, but once it reached Sujanpur, a lot of passengers got on. I was sitting on the passage side of a three-seater, almost in the middle of the bus. When a red dupatta fell on my face, I turned towards my left and saw one of the most beautiful girls on earth standing next to me. I noticed that she was wearing a black salwar suit, not the traditional Kashmiri pheran. I offered her my seat but she declined. At the next stop many people got on and the bus became quite packed. The young lady was obviously not comfortable standing. This time, when I offered her my seat, she nodded. I stood in the aisle beside her.

I finally managed to sit down after the bus had entered Jammu, and entered into a conversation with my fellow passenger. After responding to some of my more simple questions (how far my destination was, what she studied), she asked me what I did. We chatted till we reached Katra. Before she got down from the bus in Katra, I asked for her number. She gave me her landline number and told me to call if I ever came to Katra. Her name was Tanya.

It was six thirty in the evening when I got a bus to Reasi from Katra, and it was the last bus of the day. When I reached Reasi, I discovered there was no power. While searching for a phone booth from which to call my employer, I heard someone screaming my name. It was Vikash, my boss for that week. He had long hair, and was wearing his rafting attire of shorts and a T-shirt. I wondered how he had recognized me. 'You're the only one dressed like a tourist!'

My eyes fell on Vikash's Gypsy. The jeep had a raft belted down on top. Vikash introduced me to his colleagues. From the conversation, I learned that white-water rafting usually ended by seven in the evening. They had come directly from work to pick me up.

When we reached our lodging, there was still no power, so we ate our food by candlelight. Before going to bed, Vikash introduced me to Narinder who would accompany me on my morning jog the next day.

When I emerged from the building the next morning, I

saw a beautiful sunrise over the Chenab River. There was a big bridge over the river nearby and an island further down. Narinder explained that the huge building we were staying in was a recreation centre built for government, but it had not yet been handed over by the builder. Since the builder was a friend of the rafting organizers, he had allowed them to stay in it.

Narinder showed me the rafting point at the beginning of Baradari Bridge. While we jogged, he told me he was certified in many adventure sports like rafting, paragliding, and mountaineering. We crossed the bridge to the village on the other side, and then came back. Old Hindi songs were blaring from the nearest radio. The views were gorgeous and I wished that I could stay there forever.

We had breakfast at the house before departing for the day with our colleagues. Vikash was a hyperactive sort of man, the perfect guy to organize a team and get things done. His comical command to start the job was 'Oyeee chalooo oyeeee!' with a long stretched sound to every word.

The raft we would be piloting weighed around 120 kilogrammes. Together, we lifted it up and strapped it on the roof of the jeep. By nine sharp, all of us were on our way to the rafting point where we parked the Gypsy and waited for tourists to arrive. There were many vans passing by who stopped to ask us our charges for rafting.

In order to pass the time, we played cards. Whenever any tourists stopped, I would get excited, thinking that I was going to take a ride soon. 'They will do rafting while coming back, not now,' Vikash told me.

Another colleague arrived. Vikash called him Chotu, and said he was from the nearest village. Chotu is a common name in India for young people, but this Chotu was a grown man, a fearless adult who controlled the rafts despite the daunting rapids in the Chenab. Chotu had been born and brought up near the Chenab, and claimed he could cross the river on a truck tyre.

It was noon already, but not a single ride. Vikash teased me—could I swim or would I flow down the Chenab and land up in Pakistan. The river touched Pakistan at Akhnoor, 25 kilometres from our point. While I was looking at the river Vikash said, 'Let's check out your swimming skills.' He summoned everyone with a shout. 'Oyeee chalo oyeeee!' I was bit nervous but confident enough of my swimming skills.

Just below the bridge, the water was deep and the current faster thanks to the pillars. Vikash told me to wear a life jacket. The sun was high overhead, and my only thought was that at least the water be cool. 'Do you know how to swim right or should Chotu accompany you?' Vikash teased me. Before he knew it I had jumped in.

It felt like I had received an electric shock. I forgot my fear, and immediately started swimming to reach dry land. I swam for about 100 metres before I reached a spot from where I could walk back to the river bank. Till then I hadn't even noticed that Chotu had been swimming next to me. He laughed and asked me, 'How is it?' I told him it was extremely cold.

Suddenly, Vikash shouted, 'Oyeee chalo oyeeee!' seeing a group of young guys and girls stopping their cab at our point. There were three girls and four guys in the group. Some of the girls seemed nervous, and the guys were trying to convince them that it would be fun to go rafting.

Finally, three guys and two girls decided they would like to go for a ride. Vikash explained the details and negotiated the price. Once that was done, Narinder checked the safety jackets, helmets and paddles for everyone and told me to put them in the raft.

Dhiraj started the jeep, and we all set off for the starting point which was two kilometres beyond the bridge. I learned then that rafting can only be done in one direction: that in which the current is flowing. This is due to the fact that it usually takes place in areas of high turbulence. The short ride that Vikash and company offered was a three-kilometre one.

When we reached the starting point, Chotu checked the air pressure and pumped up the air in the raft. Narinder distributed the safety jackets and helmets to everyone. He instructed me on how to adjust and tighten the life jacket and to lock the helmet. Vikash gave me a waterproof bag to collect all the mobile phones, cameras and wallets so that they wouldn't get drenched. Then we all lifted the raft to take it down to the river.

Vikash organized the seating in the raft according to bodyweight so that the weight on board the raft was evenly distributed. Narinder sat at the front in the first row on the left side. Vikash told me to sit in the front row on the right side, next to Narinder. The standard practice is for the rafting staff to sit in the front and the back rows to control the direction of the raft. Most of that would happen at the back, where Vikash and Chotu sat.

Narinder instructed everyone on how to grip the foot below the front seat to avoid any kind of imbalance. Then he explained how the paddle had to be held in a 'T' grip so that the paddles wouldn't fall or hit anyone's face. He demonstrated by paddling a couple of times.

Whoever sits in front on the left is the lead paddler, and in our case that was Narinder. Vikash commanded everyone to follow the front row rider Narinder and to paddle in sync. Dhiraj left with the jeep to pick us up from the end point.

As soon as the raft set off Vikash yelled, 'Keep forward paddling till we reach the main current!' Gradually, we reached the main current.

At that point there was a steep gradient in the flow of main stream, and for the first time, water splashed over the sides of the raft. As air bubbles mixed with the water it looked almost white.

Narinder was shouting 'Ohooo! Awesome rapid!' While crossing under the bridge, we faced a big rapid. When we were about to reach the end, Vikash commanded everyone to paddle towards the river bank. Once they had completed the rafting trip safely and were back on land, all the paddlers were shouting with joy.

Vikash and Chotu got down from the raft and pulled it by the corner. The riders took out their cameras and phones to capture the moment. In the meantime, Narinder briefed me about the six grades of difficulty in white-water rafting, from the simple Class-1 rapid to the very dangerous Class-6. We had travelled between Class-3 to Class-4 rapids.

When we had driven back to the starting point, Vikash

took the charges from the riders and gave them visiting cards of the adventure club. They were damn happy with the rafting experience, as we could see from their big smiles.

With the raft firmly strapped onto the roof of the jeep we drove back to the house. Over lunch Vikash asked me what I thought of my experience. 'It was fun,' I said. 'Is that all?' Vikash laughed, so I gave him a little more insight into my experience.

Two more groups came by for rafting trips that day so I had a total of three rides on my first day. The last ride involved going to the island in the middle of the river. It was a difficult task to cross the main current to reach the island, but once we did, the island turned out to be gorgeous. Some of the customers even bathed in the water there since the current was not so strong. As we waited, Vikash told the group about the legendary folk story, *Sohni-Mahiwal*, a romance with a tragic ending that was set on the banks of the Chenab.

Mahiwal was a rich trader from Uzbekistan who fell in love with the beauty of Sohni when he saw her at her potters' shop. Instead of returning to his own country, he started working as a buffalo herder in the village, just to get a glimpse of Sohni. Once the villagers got to know about the love of Sohni and Mahiwal, her parents immediately arranged her marriage with another potter from the same community. Mahiwal eventually moved to a small hut across the river Chenab, across from Sohni's new home. Sohni could not accept her husband and every night she crossed the river to where her beloved Mahiwal herded his buffaloes. One night, her sister-in-law replaced the earthenware pot, which she used to stay afloat in the water, with a vessel of unbaked clay. The pot dissolved and she died in the whirling waves of the Chenab. Mahiwal saw Sohni drowning and jumped into the river to save her, where he perished as well.

*

I was drained and exhausted by the end of the day but helped Dhiraj cook dinner back at the house. Over a few bottles of beer, each of the rafters told me what had brought them to this line of work, and related stories of previous trips and customers. I found Dhiraj to be a very good storyteller. We also spoke about various incidents that had taken place in J&K during the major militancy period between 1988 and 2001.

Dhiraj had gone to Kerala for an NCC camp when he was in class 12. On his way home, he had stopped in Delhi. It was 1999 and the Kargil War had just begun. When he and his friends were roaming around India Gate, the Delhi police interrogated them on learning that they were from J&K. 'They suspected us of being militants, and treated us as if we were not Indian.' His anger was justified, I thought. After all, he had just served in a military camp!

They were told that they couldn't go home until the war was over. Dhiraj tried to tell the officers that the war was happening at Kargil, not in their hometown of Bhaderwah. He told me how the youth of J&K had suffered during this period.

I casually asked him, 'Why doesn't a prepaid SIM from other states work in J&K?' He replied, 'Don't you know that under Article 370 of the Indian constitution, J&K has special status. Thank god we are not being asked for our visas.'

That first day seemed to set the tone for the rest of the week. Cabs would stop by and we did get customers. Every time I went into the river, the experience was thrilling and always left me feeling thoroughly energized.

*

Since Vikash knew of my earlier marketing consultancy experience, he told me to go to Katra to market our Eco Adventures brand in the hotels and tourist guide centres. Vikash explained that basically, I had to do door-to-door sales, telling people about our adventure sports, and explain to the managers of hotels and travel agencies how they would get a commission for each tourist they sent us.

Katra reminded me at once of the beautiful girl I had met on the way. I left for Katra early in the morning, taking a bunch of Adventure Club visiting cards. By noon, I had covered all the places on my list. After that, I called Tanya. She was surprised to hear from me, and told me that she could not come out to meet me this time. Instead, she invited me to her home. Though I felt a little awkward, I noted down her address and said I would drop in.

I reached the house to find that it was located in a neighbourhood of identical quarters. A nameplate hung outside their house. I rang the bell and Tanya opened the door. She and her mother wore the traditional Kashmiri pheran embellished with distinctive embroidery. I greeted both of them, and her mother told me that they had had a puja in their home that day, and they wore traditional attire for such occasions. Tanya's father was not at home. I was told that he ran a handicrafts shop. Her mother served us green tea and went back to the kitchen.

Tanya had done her master's in sociology at Delhi University. She was very talkative and ready to chat on different topics. We discussed recent Hindi movies, and the lyrics of some of the songs. She showed me a few of her poems and articles. I thought she was quite a good poet. One of her poems was about Kashmiri Pandits, an unborn child talking about her struggle inside the womb. She spoke of how her family left Kashmir at midnight, her mother's struggle to give birth to a baby in a safe place. This sensitive issue was beautifully written.

I asked her about the genesis of the poem. Her response was, 'You would have figured from our surname Koul that we are Kashmiri Pandits.' I was not sure what to say after that. I realized from her reaction that the poem was her story. After my few minutes of silence, she restarted the conversation. She explained how her parents had struggled in the 90s, how they had to leave their village, how she was born in a refugee camp in Jammu. She told me about growing up, and finally how things got easier for them.

I learned more about the Kashmiri Pandit issue. Lakhs of Kashmiri Pandits had fled their homes; many moved to Delhi and the rest of the country. Terrorism in the Kashmir valley had begun with ethnic cleansing and the genocide of the Kashmiri Pandits between 1989 and 1990 during a period of major militancy. The majority community of the valley was mobilized by extremist Muslim leaders who supported the insurgency, leading to perhaps the biggest exodus in India since Partition.

Tanya's mother entered and said lunch was ready. The pulao, rajma, pumpkin curry, paneer and raita were all delicious, as was the chocolate barfi. I enjoyed home food after a long time.

We had had such a nice conversation that I wished I could have stayed on. Tanya invited me home again once my one-week project was over. She suggested that we could go to Vaishno Devi. I hadn't noticed the time, but once my eyes fell on the clock, I realized that I had to reach the rafting point for the afternoon rides. I told Tanya to keep in touch via mail, and to please keep up the poetry.

*

Saturday was my last day there, and I was very sure that I would miss this week for the rest of my life. I had done so much rafting, and picked up on some good techniques too. I also met Gurjeet, one of the other partners of the Adventures club. He had been away for his brother's wedding. I had landed this job through one of his friends. Gurjeet was into bodybuilding, conscious of his fitness, and looked much younger than his age. After meeting him, I could see that he and Vikash had a lot in common: they were able to make people laugh very easily.

The afternoon he arrived, Gurjeet asked me whether I had been to Derababa, our longest rafting ride of 10 kilometres. Since there were no tourists at our point, Gurjeet suggested that we head there. Our group included Vikash, Dhiraj, Chotu and his friend from the village. Narinder wanted to join in but someone had to pick us up from Derababa after the rafting.

We faced a lot of rapids on that ride. I went into my introspective mode for some time, thinking of how our lives flow with time. Today, I was living a beautiful moment, but would that ever be repeated again? Would I meet any of these people again? Would Tanya continue writing?

Dhiraj's poetic lines added flavour to those moments. After we had crossed a big rapid, he stood on the raft and loudly proclaimed, 'I love what I am doing, I don't care what people think about me. I don't know how it will happen but I am very sure that at the end of my life, I will have my own cruise and my last procession over there, without a captain.'

6. Uttarakhand

Within Miles of Devastating Floods

I was told that I might get a direct private bus to Dehradun from the Jammu interstate terminal but there didn't seem to be a single one running until late at night. Instead of wasting twelve hours just waiting for a bus, I decided to take a government interstate bus till Chandigarh and then change there.

Kuber, who ran a poly-house farm on the outskirts of Dehradun, had agreed to hire me for a week. I had had a word with him before leaving Jammu to confirm that I would be there.

It was raining so hard when I left Chandigarh that nothing was visible through the bus windows. But it turned out that the situation in Dehradun was even worse. The torrential downpour had made the bus stand non-functional. I was clueless about what to do next. My cell phone was dead and I couldn't remember if I had written down my employer's number. I figured it would be better to spend the night at a cheap hotel, charge my phone, and try to contact Kuber afterwards.

When I got down from the bus, I found the water level in the street was as high as my knee. By the time I found an auto rickshaw, I was fully drenched and so was my luggage. According to the rickshaw guy, all the hotels were full because of the heavy rains that had been pelting the city for the last two days. Most people who had planned to go to Mussoorie could not go out of Dehradun.

There wasn't a single room vacant at any of the cheap guest houses he took me to. Finally, he took me to a place that was a little way out of the city. It was a very small guest house with seven or eight rooms. One room was available upstairs. The room was decent enough for a night, and there was a common toilet just outside the room. The owner was charging thrice the usual price but I figured I would take it rather than roaming around in the rain.

After dinner at a roadside dhaba, I came back in and found a crowd around the radio at the reception. They were glued to the news coverage of the Uttarakhand floods. The headlines screamed that this was one of the worst disasters that the state had ever witnessed, the Yamuna was in spate and ten villages had been submerged. People were trapped because of the heavy landslides, and the army had commenced rescue operations to evacuate stranded pilgrims.

I hadn't spoken to my parents for weeks, and I had no idea if they were still in Uttarakhand. The landlines weren't working and I was unable to charge my phone at the reception or in the room as there was no electricity. I was extremely worried.

When a room attendant came in with a bottle of drinking

water I asked if he had a mobile phone. 'How much will you charge if I use your cell phone for one minute?' I asked the young chap. '*Ek call ka bees rupaya*,' he said. When he gave me his phone I noticed it was a Chinese brand.

My mother picked up. 'Where are you, what are you doing, when are you coming back home? Do you know what's happening in Uttarakhand?' she asked in one go. I replied that I was fine, but didn't tell her where I was. I relaxed once I heard that that they had boarded the train for Odisha from Delhi. It was strange that my mother had known about the floods in Uttarakhand even before I did, despite the fact that she was on a train!

During the course of the conversation, the boy snatched his phone back and disconnected the call since it had crossed one minute. I asked if I could make one more call, and he told that he would charge 50 rupees for both. The tariff rate of this guy's phone was more than an ISD call! I didn't have an option though, so I agreed.

Luckily I remembered that I had scribbled Kuber's number in my pocket notepad. I called to let him know that I had arrived in Dehradun. As I had expected, he complained about me not calling him earlier. It was raining heavily and his poly-house had been affected. He was planning to go visit it the next day. I was relieved when he suggested that we could go together. I didn't know much about it but from the conversation I gathered that his farm was 40 kilometres from Dehradun.

The electricity was restored that night for a few hours. The first thing I did was to charge my phone. Kuber called when he had reached my guest house the next morning. I packed my bags again and put all the wet clothes in separate polythene bags. I put my luggage in the trunk of Kuber's car and we headed to his poly-farm. The rains had abated a bit but not stopped fully.

Kuber and I were around the same age, so it didn't take much time to get friendly. One of our mutual friends had connected us when he heard about my project. Kuber was a bit formal when we started our conversation. He gave me a clearer picture of the Uttarakhand floods, saying that the rains had broken the record set 88 years back. At a rough estimate, nearly 20,000 people were still trapped in various places because of landslides and wrecked roads and bridges, most of them Chardham Yatra pilgrims. State government helicopters were being used to airlift those who had been stranded and they were being provided basic medical and other assistance. Six hanging bridges built over the Alaknanda and Mandakini rivers had also collapsed.

The involvement of the Indian Army indicated that the disaster was serious indeed. The Army was regularly reporting dead bodies recovered in various places. But the evacuation efforts kept getting disrupted due to fresh landslides in those areas. Army assistance centres had been set up to provide information, medical aid, food and water to stranded pilgrims.

Except for Dehradun and Mussoorie, most of the state had been badly affected by the floods. Due to the heavy rainfall caused by the melting of Chorabari glacier, and the eruption of the Mandakini River, there had been heavy floods. To make matters worse, two of the biggest rivers of

India originate in the region, the Ganga and the Yamuna, and both had flooded due to torrential rains.

Kuber already had my biodata based on my Facebook profile. He was a little hesitant about me staying at the poly-house farm, especially when we saw how the rains had affected the site. I convinced him not to be concerned, and thanked him. He agreed that nothing teaches one better than experience. It seems he used to spend a lot of time there when he had first started it.

When we reached the farm, it wasn't possible to drive in as the rain water had led to rills on the mud road. There was a man-made bridge of wood placed across them.

The first time I saw the poly-houses, I thought they looked like big plastic tents. As we were walking towards them, a man in his mid-fifties grinned at us. He asked Kuber, '*Saheb abhi kahan aaye aap itni baarish mein.*' He was Shantilal, the oldest worker. He had good experience with farming and horticulture. Kuber introduced me and told him that I would be working with him for a week. Given Shantilal's accent, I guessed he was from Odisha, so I asked him in Odia where he was from. It turned out that he was from Jagatsinghpur.

I would be staying with Shantilal. Two more staff members greeted Kuber who started inspecting the damage to the farm. Shantilal was asked to call the maintenance guy to replace the damaged polyethylene sheets that made up the structure of the poly-houses, called so because of the material used.

This was a time when poly-houses were getting more popular as the crops grown in them are comparatively safe from unfavourable weather conditions like heavy rain, storms, or scorching sunshine. Inside the polyethylene houses one can modify and control the environment. The Uttarakhand government had been encouraging farmers to opt for this method because of the state's fragile environment, climate, and geographical conditions. Kuber told me that the government had helped him to quite an extent.

Once Kuber had left for Dehradun, we stepped into Shantilal's quarter to keep my luggage. An asbestos roof covered the room that was about six feet wide and the same in length. It had a bamboo cot, a small metal chair, a mattress, a kerosene stove, a clay matka filled with water and a tin box in one corner. There were a few iron spikes hammered into the wall on which to hang clothes. The walls were soaked with rain water so Shantilal told me not to hang my clothes on that side. A rope was strung across from the door. I put my jeans there and changed into shorts to feel more comfortable.

Shantilal took me to the first poly-house in which beautiful gerbera flowers were blooming. The chambers were built with iron pipes and covered with thick plastic sheets. As most of the plastic sheets were three years old, one chamber had not been able to withstand the rains and hailstorm. The temperature within the poly-houses was kept cold or hot depending upon the season, and exhaust fans kept them ventilated.

I fell in love with my romantic workplace. The seeds or saplings that had been planted in April were just beginning to bloom. There was fungus in a few plants because of overwatering. My first task was to remove old leaves to prevent fungal infections. Shantilal told me to remove the old leaves from alternate rows of plants; he would do the rest.

The gerbera is a thirty-month crop and blooms throughout the year. It was beautiful to see an abundance of flowers in an area of less than one square metre. Two days later the rain diminished and flower collectors arrived to harvest the blossoms. They are usually plucked early in the morning or evening, when the temperature is low.

After harvesting, the flowers were sorted according to the size of the bud and colour. To avoid damaging the stem during transportation, the flowers were packed into ten flowers per bunch. We tied them with rubber bands and packed them in separate boxes according to the colour.

One evening, I made Odia dalma, a popular dish of vegetables, lentils and spices, and rice. After eating the last bite, Shantilal happily declared that it was good to taste someone else's cooking. 'I was bored of my own cooking,' he declared. He asked me how I knew how to make dalma, since it was popular in eastern Odisha and I'm from the west. I explained that I had learned the preparation during my college days.

When I asked Shantilal how long it had been since he went to his village, he didn't say anything for a while. And then he shared his story. He had lost his family in the 1999 super cyclone when his home district was badly affected. He had escaped the devastation as he had been in Chennai, working as a lease labourer. When he returned, it was to find that his wife and daughter had passed away.

I felt very sorry for having asked the question. He asked me, 'Do you know why we pray to Jagannath?' Without understanding the depth of his question I replied that it was because his name suggests he is the God of the world, Jagannath.

He nodded. There are many interpretations of why Jagannath's form is depicted the way it is, incomplete. Shantilal shared a beautiful one. In ancient times the tribal people who lived in the forests and on the mountains usually prayed to the tree as God. Even Jagannath was considered as the god of a specific scheduled tribe called Shabar. And if you look at the huge form of Jagannath, there are no palms, feet or ears. Only the forehead, eyes and nose are painted on the trunk of a tree. In the name of modernization, we started cutting down trees, resulting in natural disasters like the super cyclone and the Uttarakhand floods. These disasters happened because of our sins, he said.

Shantilal brought me an English newspaper from the guy who handled the control system of the poly-houses. The number of deaths from the flood had risen. More than 5,000 people were presumed dead and 100,000 pilgrims were trapped in the valleys leading to the Chota Char Dham. The Indian Air Force, the Indian Army, and paramilitary troops had evacuated more than 110,000 people from the flood-ravaged area.

There was an article that featured Bollywood superstars tweeting about the Uttarakhand floods. Many members from the Hindi film fraternity, including megastars Amitabh Bachchan and Shahrukh Khan, Javed Akhtar and others were mourning the current situation in Uttarakhand. The king of Bollywood, Shahrukh Khan, was quoted as saying, 'As insignificant as we are against Nature's fury, a prayer of Hope for all suffering in Uttarakhand. May Allah give them strength and safety.'

7. Haryana

Capturing Ethnic Weaves on Camera

Before heading for Mumbai, the city of dreams, I had a confirmed job with a company in Gurgaon. It was one of the very first offers I got after some leading entrepreneurship portals covered my job-hopping journey.

I had received an email from Rahul Narvekar, the CEO of NDTV's Ethnic Retail division. He had asked me to drop by his office. The NDTV group had opened an e-commerce portal for the sale of ethnic clothes. It was called Indianroots.com.

I reached the office thirty minutes before the scheduled time. Indianroots.com was at its incipient stage, and had a start-up vibe. There were lots of energetic, enthusiastic people walking around. I waited for a few minutes outside the CEO's cabin, and soon Rahul called me inside.

Rahul poured more energy into my journey as he had obviously grasped what I was trying to do. He asked me what would interest me more, the post of a CEO or that of a chaiwallah. I was happy that he understood the other aspect of the whole journey—that of suppressing my ego and working at any kind of job.

It was decided that my designation would be that of a visual content creator. Indianroots.com was gradually expanding, listing their stock of ethnic clothes on their website, and collaborating with designers and manufacturers from across the country. My job was to collect visual content for the portal.

My first day was spent learning some basic photography techniques. I was introduced to the use of a professional camera. The instrument fascinated me. I was handed an assignment: photographing handlooms and rare crafts of the Kurukshetra region.

This is a place that is known to every Indian, as the Kurukshetra war of the Mahabharata was fought on this land. This is the very place of the holy Bhagavad Gita.

As I walked down a street in Kurukshetra, I passed a few handloom weavers. Diwan sets, dohars, bedsheets and curtains were lined up perfectly in rows under the bright sun. The weavers themselves sold their wares. I took lots of pictures.

Soon, a few malnourished, barely dressed kids had surrounded me. Their families wove clothes for others, but not enough to cover the bodies of their own children. Most of them wanted me to take their picture. One of them asked, 'When will we get the photo?' 'Tomorrow,' I said, grinning.

A sweet female voice said, 'He is making a fool out of you; he won't give you any pictures. All of them are the same.' I turned to see a teenage girl gazing at me, combing her hair as she sat on a broken plastic stool. She was fair and beautiful with sharp, round eyes. I felt like her eyes could read my thoughts. 'Take a picture of me,' she said. 'I want to see how I look.' I clicked a few pictures and before putting my camera down to show her the shots, I had a glimpse of them myself. She had a beautiful smile. Her mother was sleeping next to her. She woke her up and asked me if I could click one more with her mother. Her mother was weak and looked older than she actually was. She tied her grey hair into a bun to pose for the photo. I smiled at them and clicked a few more.

The next day, Lakshya, my companion and guide, and I were heading to a professional photoshoot. A model would be wearing some of the clothes to be displayed on the company site. I was supposed to assist the photographer at the studio.

I had never seen a photoshoot of this kind before. A beautiful model posed, flaunting the ethnic wear in different postures. She looked attractive in all of the outfits. Every time she changed her clothes, she changed her make-up as well. The lipstick sometimes matched the colour of the attire, and the tone of her face looked different each time. The photographer made the model feel comfortable with his witty jokes, and created a jovial environment that made us forget about the tiring task at hand.

During one of the breaks, the model was smoking a cigarette. I pulled up a chair next to her. I wanted to start a conversation but I was clueless about what to say. We sat in silence for a few minutes and exchanged glances. She offered me a smoke. I took a puff gladly. After some time I said 'Quite a day!' She nodded and sighed, exhausted. Her name was Samikshya, and she was a student of English Honours at

Miranda House, Delhi. She confessed that the photoshoot for the e-commerce portal was more hectic than a fashion show. But it offered good money. When she learned that my native state was Odisha, she told me excitedly that she was a trained Odissi dancer and had even visited the state the previous year.

Odissi is a beautiful classical dance form from Orissa. There is a village called Raghurajpur near Puri where one can learn the original dance form, Gotipua. Gotipua is a strange form whose practitioners create an illusion: that they are all part of a single body. Samikshya asked whether I had visited Raghurajpur. I was ashamed to say that I hadn't as yet, but I had heard a lot about pattachitra, its traditional paintings on cloth.

The one-day photoshoot stretched to two days. My last day at Indianroots was spent in front of a computer screen, watching the photographer do all the finishing tasks to make the pictures look more appealing.

Rahul called me when I was about to leave the office. He gave me a few contacts for my journey ahead. He asked me whether I would be working on a Bollywood movie in Mumbai. 'You should work as a lemonade seller under the Dadar station to feel the real Bombay,' he suggested. I nodded and smiled.

*

I was staying with my engineering classmate, Jeeban. He suggested I book a tatkal ticket to Mumbai. This is a special feature offered by Indian Railways for last minute travellers, which allows them to book a ticket 24 hours before their journey at any railway station booking office or via internet reservation. Booking online was almost impossible as when the booking would open at ten in the morning, the IRCTC site usually went down due to heavy traffic. By the time one landed on the last webpage to confirm a ticket, the session would have either expired or all the tickets would have been sold out.

Those looking to book tatkal tickets would queue up from the early hours of the morning although the booking counters opened at ten. Jeeban had done some 'fixing' with a ticket broker a day in advance so I didn't have to wake up too early. I reached Okhla railway station at eight in the morning and called the broker. I had expected to meet the guy who was to have booked my ticket, but instead I was presented with a different experience altogether.

A chaiwallah answered my call while serving tea to his customers. In a very low voice, he told me to head to his tea stall and approach him when there were no customers. I watched the tea stall from 30 feet away; it looked like any other tea stall in a small town.

I went to the tea counter when there were no customers around, and the guy handed me a cup of tea without asking whether I wanted it or not. He told me that I should join the queue at nine and stand fifth in the line—I would be replacing one of his chaps appointed for the job. I was to tell the man at the counter that my name was Ravi and that my father had been standing in line for me. He had gone home now to freshen up, so I would be taking his place.

The whole story was made up to placate those who saw a new face in the crowd. At the end, the chaiwallah told me, 'Don't worry, *humara SETTING hai andar bhi.*' He showed me a paper which listed the names of all those who were standing in line for tickets. The first five names belonged to those who were at the tea stall.

How the system worked was that before people started arriving in the early hours to stand in the line, this paper would be given to the chaiwallah who would write down random names for his customers. It was then given to the actual aspirants. A policeman checked everyone's names before distributing the reservation form and writing a number on it.

The policeman rechecked the names individually, and helped the crowd to maintain the queue. I was ready to give my fake name Ravi. But strangely, the fifth name was marked and my real name was there. I stood quietly and looked at the chaiwallah, and he nodded at me. In India 'setting' is synonymous with corruption. We resort to it when we are desperate.

There were five counters at the railway station and the police helped maintain some order. When the clock struck ten, everyone was alert and tense. The man at the counter tried his best to type in the passenger information as quickly as possible. He checked my identity proof, took the money, and finally gave me the ticket. As I walked away, I noticed people staring at me, muttering that I had been very lucky.

It was only when I came outside that I learned just how much this 'setting' would cost me. The chaiwallah passed me another cup of tea, and trying to justify his guilt, said,

'*Saheb kya karein, sabki mazburi hota hai.*' He pointed to an older couple who were walking away from his tea stall, smiling widely. He explained that they had been unable to secure tickets to Mumbai and had to get there for a medical check-up, and he had helped them out.

When I smiled at him and asked how much the tea cost, he said it was 400 rupees. He had included his price for the 'setting' as well. I paid up with no argument. It must have been the most expensive tea I'd ever had in my life.

8. Maharashtra

A Taste of Bollywood with the Lootera Stars

Heading out to a job from home is a different experience. Staying at my sister's place in Mumbai, I was very relaxed as I didn't have to worry about washing my clothes or figuring out what to eat. My brother-in-law, a serious person and sincere about his job, was a research scientist in a pharmaceutical laboratory. He left for work at nine, right after breakfast. He was probably one of the few people in Mumbai whose office was within walking distance. He would usually come home for lunch too.

My four-year-old niece would turn on the TV as soon as her father left for work. She would flip through the music channels. My sister complained about her daughter's excessive fondness for Bollywood songs. We spoke about our childhood days when the only way to listen to film songs was through musical programmes like *Rangoli* or *Chitrahaar*, which only aired once a week on Doordarshan.

People seem to believe that life in Mumbai is the fastest and the most happening kind, based on what they see on screen. Since my childhood, I had had a fascination for the city and wanted to settle down there—that is, until I actually saw what the real Mumbai was like.

Whenever I visited this city of dreams, my walking speed doubled and my confidence levels increased. It's a city of dreamers; everybody works hard with dreams of success. It is one of those cities where I have seen people driven by their dreams.

I was well acquainted with the western line of the Mumbai local train as I had worked there. I used to stay in Malad, and my office was in Bandra. My friend Pavan loved to stand near the door of the local train to get some fresh air, so we would hang on to the iron railing inside. It had been a year since those days, and here I was again travelling in the same local. Like every Mumbaikar my bag was hanging from my chest to make it easy to move inside the packed train. This time though I would travel a shorter distance as my office was in Vile Parle.

SPICE, a leading Bollywood public relations firm, builds brands for top celebrities and designs communication strategies for movies. I had received the offer to be a marketing executive through Gurvinder, my roommate during my Mumbai days. We had discussed this role multiple times.

In movie marketing, a simple idea is executed and communicated in such a way that it touches people's hearts. I enjoyed some of the stories and ideas. During the release of *Bodyguard*, Salman Khan's personal bodyguard Shera became a communication high point and achieved celebrity status. The village towel *gamcha* was used as a promotional tool during *Gangs of Wasseypur*, and Aamir Khan gave *Ghajini*-style haircuts to common people in a crowded Bengali market area of New Delhi.

Very few people know about the importance of the right PR consultants and their role in the success of a movie. The relationship between PR firms and film production companies is a low-key one. The PR consultant is one of the reasons behind the success of a film, but they can't talk about it. SPICE became very popular in Bollywood for its successful handling of brands, huge stars like Aamir Khan and Deepika Padukone, and communication strategies for many big films like *Ghajini, Delhi Belly, 3-Idiots, Ek Tha Tiger* and *Bodyguard*.

Almost every big film listed SPICE as a media consultant. I would look for the SPICE logo whenever I went to the movies. I would always tell the person seated next to me in the theatre that my friend worked for SPICE. Starting that week I would be able to boast about myself!

I reached the office a little early on my first day. Sunil was the only one there. He was busy with a bundle of newspapers and magazines at his desk and a scanner next to the pile. Gurvinder might have told him about me, because when I introduced myself he was welcoming and didn't look surprised. We had a short conversation and he went back to work. When I asked him why there were two copies of many of the newspapers, he was happy to share that it was his duty to scan all the stories of the company's clients and their competitors. In order to not miss any important articles on the other side of a cut page, the company subscribed to two copies of every newspaper and magazine.

I was meeting Gurvinder after a year and for the first time since he got married. The careless bachelor had become quite the married man. I pulled his leg when I saw the lunch box in his bag. This was the same guy who would make our daily dinner bills run up to nearly a thousand rupees simply because he always wanted to have good food in a nice restaurant. He took my teasing in the right spirit. 'You'll be lunching with me as your Bhabiji has packed food for both of us.'

I got a laptop set up next to Gurvinder's desk. He was working on SPICE Bhasha, which dealt exclusively with Bollywood movie promotions in the Tier-2 cities. He said that revenues from the small towns had become a major source of returns for the Hindi film industry. The bulk of the viewers were now from the Tier-2 cities and northern India, no longer Mumbai and the western states. Many movies were now based in those regions to reflect this.

By this time, the office had become full and lively. Movie projects and big celebrity names were being bandied about casually, as though the speakers were talking about close friends.

I was more curious to meet Prabhat Choudhary, the founder of SPICE PR and the 'god' of Indian film marketing, than to meet a movie star. People go crazy about their favourite stars, but I was more interested in knowing about the person who could convert a name into a celebrity, a signature into an autograph. I had done a thorough Google search and scrutinized the major social networking sites like Facebook and Twitter the day before, and found it very strange that I could dig up nothing on Prabhat. He kept himself out of all Bollywood media events, parties, and minimized his online presence. I had not found a single image of him in Google image search either.

The general perception of those working in marketing and PR is that these people are extroverted and enjoy socializing and networking. But the PR guru of Bollywood was exceptional; he did not need to prove his connections. I didn't even realize it was Prabhat when a six foot-tall gentleman entered the office and sat calmly in his chair in the middle of the room. In my previous corporate experiences, I had noted that employees usually behaved differently once the boss had entered the office. Here, the scenario was different. I quite liked the environment and culture of the office. People seemed to be working because they loved their job, and not getting distracted from their tasks.

When Gurvinder introduced me to Prabhat his first question was whether I wanted to set a Guinness record by doing so many jobs in India. He was very soft-spoken, and always smiled irrespective of what he said. He and Gurvinder discussed the communication strategy they were planning for the upcoming flick *Shuddh Desi Romance*. In between, he asked who had gone for the interview of *Lootera*. He suggested I should go to get the basic idea of my job for the week.

It was my first day in the office and I was going for a press conference! Gurvinder told me the venue was Taj Lands' End, Bandra, near Shahrukh Khan's bungalow, Mannat. I took an auto to reach the place. At the security check, I introduced myself as a journalist for the *Lootera* interview. I could have told them my real identity and that I was from SPICE, but this had become a habit. Claiming to be from the press had given me entry to many events during my student days. The security guard told me the event was happening in the Malabar Meeting Room.

Purvi was the only other person from SPICE at the event. It was her job to act as the liaison between the media and the stars. I had seen her at the office earlier that morning, but we hadn't had a chance to introduce ourselves. She recognized me and gave me a brief of the event. In the middle of our chat she took a call from a journalist and rushed towards the conference room. Purvi had recently graduated with a degree in Mass Communication from Mumbai University. She seemed eager and happy with the job.

Purvi had organized one-on-one interviews with every news channel; first would be the Hindi news channels and later the English ones. Inside the conference room, there were teams present from every major news channel; the teams comprised a journalist and a cameraman. Most of the reporters' faces were familiar as I had seen them on TV.

There was a representative from Balaji Productions to handle the logistics of the event. Inside the meeting room, there were two interview set-ups with big flex standees featuring posters of *Lootera* positioned behind each one. The stars were yet to arrive.

The world runs on perception. We create a perception of the human beings we have met or seen in our lives. Similarly, we create an image of a film star after watching them on the big screen and television, or by reading about them in newspapers and magazines. While actors have several roles in their lives, it's difficult for the common man to draw a line between the actor's reel self and real self. For instance, I had built up my own impression of Ranveer Singh after watching him play a typical Delhi University boy in *Band*

Baaja Baaraat and a conman in his second film, *Ladies Vs Ricky Bahl*. When I finally saw Ranveer, I realized that, contrary to the image I had built up in my mind, he seemed a friendly, fun-loving guy, full of energy.

The first interview was about to start. The cameraman set his frame on the reporter's face. She was a young Bollywood reporter, quite a well-known face, wearing a dashing outfit. Sonakshi Sinha, the other star of the film, was in much simpler attire: jeans and a white jacket. Ranveer was in jeans, white shirt and a sky blue blazer. He had a beard now, part of his look for the character he was playing in his next film, *Ramleela*. Once the cameraman muttered 'Rolling', the reporter had her mike ready to start the interview and simultaneously the camera started moving towards Ranveer and Sonakshi.

The reporter's introduction was a blooper. She started by saying, 'I am here with the pair about town, Sonakshi Singh and Ranveer ... cut cut cut!' She giggled at her mistake. 'I said Sonakshi Singh. Sorry.' Sonakshi shrugged and smiled, while Ranveer tried to make a joke by saying 'Sonakshi Singh and Ranveer Sinha!' The reporter giggled again and requested the cameraman to restart the roll.

After that the interview went smoothly. There were general questions about the shooting experience, and then the reporter asked Ranveer about his conman characters in two consecutive films. Before Ranveer could answer, Sonakshi tried to pull his leg. '*Iski toh sakal pe hi likha hai,*' she said, meaning he is a born *lootera*.

At the end of the interview, the reporter requested the stars to act out the famous song *Sawar Loon* from the movie.

Ranveer sang while Sonakshi did a few steps of the dance. My guess was that when the video reached the editor's desk they would add in the original song to make the whole interview more impactful.

During the interview for India TV both Sonakshi and Ranveer became more melodramatic. It included a rapid answer round about how well they knew each other's likes and dislikes. There was a moment when Ranveer had to present a flower to Sonakshi. She left the room but came back almost at once and grabbed the flower, saying '*Bahut slow hai yaar, dede bhi flower*!' This was one of the funniest moments of the day. I began to visualize the headline on the news channels: 'What's cooking between Ranveer and Sonakshi?' I was damn sure that when I reached home that evening, my sister would ask if there something going on between the two stars.

Ranveer was peppy throughout. There were just a few more interviews left for the English channels. The make-up artists gave a touch up to both the actors before the next round. All went smoothly till the last one when Purvi asked the reporter to keep the interview short as both the stars had to leave for some other promotional events. Being from the PR industry, which acts as the intermediary between the media and the stars, Purvi could not force the journalists to heed her words. But the lady from the production house bluntly told the journalist that she should complete the interview with just two questions. The journalist responded furiously, 'Better we don't do the interview then.' The lady from the production house said not more than five minutes but the journalist insisted on ten minutes.

Ranveer loves to talk to the media, and he extended the interview. As it drew out, the production house lady kept butting in every time the journalist asked another question. Ranveer held the crowd's attention with his good PR skills and friendly approach. My image of him as a conman was gone forever.

As films in India usually release on Fridays, these press conferences were organized in the week leading upto it. After the conferences, the leading pair would go on a city tour to generate as much buzz as possible in order to boost sales at the cinema halls. In the case of *Lootera*, the first press meet was on a Monday. Over the following days, Ranveer and Sonakshi were on promo tours in Ahmedabad, Jaipur, Indore and Kolkata. A colleague from SPICE went with them, and he sent me pictures and other visuals.

I handled a digital campaign on Facebook called 'Meet the *Lootera* stars'. Gurvinder guided me on the kind of quiz questions I could pose about the stars to their fan following. Responses flooded in as there was a lucky draw. The prize was a meeting with the stars and getting photographed with them. Such Facebook campaigns would go viral during the release as youngsters were crazy about meeting their favourite stars. I loved my job and was learning a lot about the Bollywood-crazy segment.

Prior to a movie's release, the chief communication points are deliberated upon and decided. One of my days at SPICE was packed with discussions about a film which was on the editing table and due to be released in six months. It was a movie directed by Neeraj Pandey. Friday Film Works,

Pandey's company, had held a special screening for a SPICE team. Post the screening, we were conducting a brainstorming session on the brand positioning of the movie.

Neeraj Pandey had come into the limelight after his critically acclaimed *A Wednesday*. The movie, which portrayed a common man's revenge for the Mumbai train bombings, became very popular. In his latest film, the leading actors were Ali Zafar as Aman, a Pakistani boy, and Yami Gautam as Asha, an Indian girl. They fall in love in London and want to get married. Aman visits her parents' house to seek their permission. Chaos unfolds. The initial title of the movie was *Aman Ki Asha*.

Whether the title suited the movie was one of the key points raised in our in-house discussion. Prabhat asked everyone at the meeting what their first thoughts were when the name was mentioned to them. For me, 'Aman Ki Asha' brought to mind a very popular campaign with the same name run by the *Times of India*, which aimed for peace between India and Pakistan. One person agreed with me, saying that the name had a connection with an earlier campaign, and as it was about a love story between two countries, it was perfect for the movie.

Prabhat had a different point of view. What made the film *Gadar* a hit? Some said it was due to the fan following of Sunny Deol's muscular heroic figure, others said it was the cross-border romance shown in the film. Prabhat's take was that viewers had an emotional reaction to a man who would go to Pakistan for his love, fight with the whole army and come back with his wife and kid. That was the recipe for success. People went crazy over Sunny Deol. While the plot of *Gadar* was based on the Partition of 1947, *Aman Ki Asha* as a title would perhaps not ring true for the masses.

We discussed what could be done to promote the film. Purvi suggested that we take a cue from Coca Cola's cross-border 'Open happiness' campaign. That was a very popular advertising campaign that showed vending machines installed at shopping malls in New Delhi and Lahore. People on both sides of the border were invited to make a friend in the other country, and to share a Coca-Cola. It had a large 3D touch screen to do a friendly task together like wave, touch hands, create a friendly symbol, or dance. And at the end the machine dispensed a can of Coca-Cola.

Everyone in the meeting room got excited about that idea. Prabhat took his time to react and then with a big sigh he said, 'Don't paint a portrait, paint a landscape. Never think about an individual, think about an organization, and from a corporate prospective. Think about the big picture. Can we sell the film with such an idea? Do you think that will touch the audience in small town single-screen theatres? Do you really think they would see it as practical for an Indian girl to get married to a Pakistani boy?' When someone gave the example of Indian tennis player Sania Mirza and Pakistani cricketer Shoaib Malik, Prabhat agreed that there could be some exceptions.

Gurvinder suggested that Yami Gautam's family organize a dinner party for Ali Zafar at their Chandigarh home as a reflection of what her character does in the movie. The dinner idea was accepted by everyone, including Prabhat. It was decided that *Aman ki Asha* did not really encompass the lighter side of the movie and the comical chaos that happened during the dinner. The movie released as *Total Siyappa*, meaning total chaos.

By the time we wrapped up work, it was raining outside. Gurvinder had left much earlier that day. Some of my colleagues were heading to the Excel entertainment office for a party they were throwing to celebrate the success of the movie *Fukrey*. I had heard from friends that it was a youth-centric film which appealed to youngsters. I tagged along to the party, hoping to meet a few Bollywood stars.

Purvi, Sanjeevani and I took an auto to the Excel office. Sanjeevani was handling the PR for *Fukrey*, and on the way, she gave us a few insights into the movie's promotion. A beautiful girl with glowing skin, brightly coloured lips, sparkling eyes and a girlish gait got into the lift with us. She smiled at me. I wondered who she was.

Before we could step out of the lift on the sixth floor, around ten over-enthusiastic photographers rushed forward to click pictures of the beautiful lady. I joined Sanjeevani and asked her who she was. The beautiful lady with whom I had shared the lift and exchanged a smile was none other than the actress from *Fukrey*, Vishakha Singh.

Aside from the leading stars, writer and director of the film, there weren't many people. Of course there were a few Bollywood reporters with their crew. I had seen most of them at the *Lootera* press conference. A few of them started talking to me, accepting me as a new member of their tribe.

I was enjoying myself and wished I could continue with my job in the glamour world for a bit longer.

My next assignment at SPICE was at their screening of *Lootera* for the media at PVR Juhu. The screenings for the media are usually held a day before the movie's public release so that they would have enough time to write advance reviews for the general public.

Sukesh, my partner for the day, was a senior employee of the company and knew almost every print media journalist, TV reporter, photographer, camera crew, RJ, VJ, and the new digital media journalists. We were at the front desk, distributing tickets to those who presented their media IDs. There were many youngsters as well, all representing new sites on Bollywood. I was told to keep a record of their details for the next movie screening.

A senior journalist started shouting when he was asked for his identity card. 'First you call me for the screening then you ask who I am!' The truth was that the company sent a mass message to the media, and not individual invitations. Sukesh calmed him down by giving him a ticket.

We rushed into the hall just before the screening. A whole row was occupied by the SPICE team. It was the first time I was watching a movie with the top critics of Bollywood.

Lootera was a visual masterpiece, and I loved the background score. I had not expected such overwhelming performances from Ranveer and Sonakshi. The character development of Sonakshi's role was superb and when the love story took a tragic twist, I savoured the poetry of the lyrics that played:

Kya kabhi savera laata hai andhera
Sukhi syahi deti hai gavaahi
Sadiyon purani aisi ek kahaani
Reh gayi reh gayi ... Ankahee

Finally, judgment day arrived: Friday, the most important day for the stakeholders in the film industry. Every major newspaper had a story about *Lootera*, thanks to our office. By afternoon, after the first day's first show screening in theatres all over India, all the social media like Facebook and Twitter were flooded with reviews. Many people in the media talked about Sonakshi and Ranveer, wondering whether there was any romance cooking between them.

At the office everyone was talking about the different reviews. Prabhat interrupted saying, 'We have done our job, let the audience do theirs. We are from the land of the Buddha. We are all good preachers, but not good followers. When it comes to cricket, Bollywood or politics in India, everyone thinks they are themselves a critic. We are all good at that.'

Prabhat asked about my next destination. I told him it was Goa. 'Beaches, fancy cars, no parental supervision and romance with an American girl made every Indian teenager want to go to Goa.' He was referring to the impression youngsters had of Goa from *Dil Chahta Hai*, the hugely successful film his firm had handled.

9. Goa

Each Tattoo Has a Story to Tell

Goa was the first state where I did not have a single contact. I had a few friends at a management institute there but no connections to work openings. I would have to look for a job once I got there.

While my sister was calling me to dinner, I checked my email again. I was surprised to see a mail from Janessa, the girl I had met in Himachal. It was brief. 'I am in Goa, find me if you can' was the subject line with no text in the body of the mail.

I boarded the Mangalore Express from the Chhatrapati Shivaji Terminus that night. Thanks to the rain and a slight fever, I fell asleep easily. A fellow passenger on the train woke me when we were about to reach Madgaon. When I gathered my luggage, I saw there was a big hole in one of my bags. Clearly, it had been chewed up by a rat.

The view from the window was beautiful. It was the monsoon season and everything looked so green and lush. At the taxi stand, someone informed me that it would cost nearly a thousand bucks to reach Panjim. I just laughed at the idea of spending three times what it had cost me to travel from Mumbai to Goa.

I was looking for a cheaper alternative when a guy on a bike asked if I wanted a drop to the bus stand. I thought he was offering me a ride as a hitchhiker, but discovered it was a paid transportation service called Pilot. These bikers usually drop you wherever you want in Goa at a reasonable price. The guy put my luggage on the petrol tank, and I sat on the pillion seat.

He dropped me to Kadamba bus stand from where I got a bus to Panjim. I found a seat on the bench at the back of the bus, where I was joined by a few more travellers.

On the 30-kilometre journey from Madgaon to Panjim we drove past white buildings in the Portuguese style, through narrow streets and lush, leafy groves—a refreshing change from the hustle and bustle of Mumbai. I overheard two of my fellow passengers saying that this was the off-season in Goa, with very few tourists during the monsoon. I told myself that I had come at the perfect time.

As soon as I got down at Panjim, a guy approached me to ask if I needed to rent a bike. The rent was a reasonable sum of 200 rupees per day. He asked for a copy of my Pan Card as security and two days' rent in advance. Then I kick-started the bike and took off to find my two Js: Janessa, and a job.

Candolim beach was my first destination. It was not crowded. There were a few vendors selling printed T-shirts with Bob Marley's face, colourful bags and trinkets made of seashells. A woman was offering to do *mehendi* or henna tattoos. I declined her offer, but it ignited an idea.

Much before my trip to Goa I had contacted a tattoo artist to ask if he would hire me but he had refused. I figured I would ask a few more if they would take me on as an apprentice. I also looked at every foreigner I came across while roaming around the beach, passing through guest houses, and in small shops, checking to see if I could spot Janessa. Each time, my search ended in disappointment.

I sat down for some time on Calangute beach, looking at the waves. An old saffron-attired sadhu baba came up to me and asked if I wanted weed.

I headed towards Baga for a beer at a shack on the beach. Baga beach is dotted with hundreds of shacks with very little to distinguish one from the other. There was a hoarding advertising Club Tito's. I had heard about Tito's from my friends, who said that it was one of the most happening places in Goa. I thought that if I could get a job on the lane to Tito's, it would increase my chances of meeting Janessa. I remembered that she had mentioned how much she loved this club.

Although I wasn't very optimistic, I entered the Inkbaba Tattoo Studio in the Tito's lane. Instead of asking for a job, I walked in like any customer might and looked at the tattoo patterns in the albums.

Manish, the young tattoo artist there, told me about his journey in tattooing. His artistic nature had blossomed at a very young age. When he was in school, he had come to the media's attention for writing around 100 letters on one grain of rice. He explained how tattooing had become very commercial in Goa, which devalued its artistry and his creative instincts. He showed me some of his sketches and challenged me, 'If you get better finished tattoos than the ones I create here, I will do this work for free for the rest of my life.'

His attitude really touched me and I didn't want to miss out on the opportunity to gain experience at this studio. Later, he showed me some of the works of his boss, Sachin Aarote, the founder of the studio. Sachin, a very popular tattoo artist in Bollywood, had a studio in Mumbai with the same name. He divided his time between Goa and Mumbai.

Luckily Sachin was there and soon joined us. When I spoke about my One Week Job project, he thought it was a cool idea and took me on to assist him.

The two artists were quite different by nature. While Manish was very chatty, Sachin was the opposite. Manish had five ear-piercings but there were no visible tattoos or piercings on Sachin.

The studio attracted more customers at night, when Tito's was in full swing, so they opened late in the afternoon and kept it open till midnight. When I told them about my quest to find Janessa, Sachin thought it was very romantic as well as filmy. He told me to go to Arambol beach to look.

I was to start work that evening so I left my luggage there and headed out on my bike. Arambol is a pretty beach filled with a kaleidoscope of humanity: idealistic teenagers, born-again oldies, hippies, cannabis addicts in their altered states of consciousness, colourful foreigners and Indian vendors. Some were practising yoga, some were lounging and others looked like they were trying to get a spiritual high by dancing to trance music. It looked like they were all friends even if they hadn't exchanged names.

I looked around but couldn't spot Janessa.

A tanned man with a white beard was selling jewellery made of seashells, trinkets and semi-precious pendants. He looked like a hippie poster boy from the 1960s in a worn brown jacket, dazzling rings on his fingers and dreadlocks. We struck up a conversation. He said his name was Martin, aged 60, and was from the UK.

Goa had become a popular hippie destination. Travellers would take an overland route through Europe, Greece, Turkey, Afghanistan and Pakistan and then arrive in India. Martin described it as the hippie trail. In Indian history texts this route is referred to as the Badshah road which connected foreign lands with the oldest city, Pataliputra. When Martin reached Goa and saw the wonderland of Anjuna, he decided to stay put.

Martin was humming the Beatles' song, *All you need is love*. In today's competitive world, here was a hippie who was welcoming to everyone, and was happy to be in a place of peace and harmony.

By the time I got back to the Inkbaba studio in the evening, the Tito's lane was buzzing with comings and goings. I parked my bike at the end of the lane facing the beach and walked back to the tattoo studio. I was a bit confused about whether I had come to the right place since it looked so different at night. Everyone was in a party mood, and the smell of alcohol was so strong that it overpowered the natural smell of the sea. High decibel music was coming out of the café opposite the studio.

A firangi girl was leaving the tattoo studio as I walked in. Sachin was trying to pull my leg. 'Janessa came here looking for you.' I commented on how lively and different the lane looked. Manish said, 'Nights are very different and the evening has just begun. Plus today is Sunday night. Just wait and watch!'

I could see two black-shirted bouncers standing in the rear lane. My eyes fell on the words on their T-shirts: Everything happened over a drink. I smiled, thinking about the three strata of urbanization in India: a small town where nothing may happen over a glass of water, Tier-2 cities where a lot can happen over a cup of coffee, and here in night clubs where everything can happen over a drink or a cup of coffee.

In small towns, asking for a glass of water during awkward moments can be an ice-breaker. This often happens when a boy and a girl are introduced by families with the hope of settling their marriage. The guy usually asks for a glass of water, the girl passes the glass with a smile and the guy smiles back. And nothing happens afterwards other than an innocent exchange of feelings.

In café culture, a lot can happen over a cup of coffee. It ranges from the first meeting to endless talk. And here, things move two steps faster in the nightclubs: everything can happen over a drink which could even lead to the three-letter magical word of sex.

It was time to work. Sachin gave me a basic introduction

to the elements of tattooing: tattoo inks, tattoo machine, and hygiene procedures. Before going further, he tested my sketching skills by asking me to do a painting of any Indian mythological character. I hadn't painted in a long time, more than five years. The last time was when I had done a portrait of Sameen, to honour my first love.

During my schooldays I used to paint 'Navagunjara'. That was the first mythological character that popped into my mind. It is the omni-form of Lord Krishna, which he displays to Arjuna in the Bhagavad Gita, as described by the poet Sarala Dasa in the Odia Mahabharata. In Navagunjara, the *Vishwaroopa* or universal form of Krishna is shown as a creature composed of a human form with eight different animals: rooster, elephant, tiger, deer, horse, peacock, bull and snake.

Sachin was very impressed by my drawing. 'This is very different,' he said. This particular depiction was not popular outside Odisha, so he was seeing it for the first time. He was so carried away by the character that he ignored the mistakes in my painting.

During our discussion, a newly-married couple entered the studio. The guy already had a tattoo on his forearm. It looked as though a kid had exacted his revenge by putting ugly black lines on his arm. He wanted to cover the mess up with a new tattoo. Manish asked him what he wanted in place of the Buddha, but I had assumed it was a Shiva. His wife corrected us and said it was a Ganesha. It was strange that the characteristic elephant trunk was missing!

Sachin asked where he had had the tattoo done. They were

from Jhansi and he had got it done during a festival in the city. A post-tattoo infection had made it even more horrible.

Sachin said that in some parts of rural India, the artists used hair dye as tattoo ink. Even in Goa, a few street tattoo guys used it. The dye combined with poor hygiene standards resulted in all kinds of problems such as allergic reactions and an elevated risk of infection.

Manish noted the man's requirement and quoted a price of 3,000 rupees. The guy retorted that he had paid 200 rupees the last time. After they had left the studio, Sachin pointed out the risks involved in tattooing. 'No matter how good you are at sketching, I won't allow you to experiment on anyone's skin.' I respected his sticking to his principles and agreed to do the menial tasks in the studio instead. I would watch and wait for a few days even before experimenting on the fake skin he said I could practise on.

A group of three girls entered our studio around eleven that night. All three of them had some peculiar lightning hair bands, and the smell of alcohol was strong. One of them wanted a tattoo of her boyfriend's name on her wrist.

This was my first live tattooing session. Once the girl gave us her boyfriend's name, Sachin drew a design of it and added a few butterflies above it. The girl loved the design. Manish prepared the ink, the tattoo machine, and the disposable needle. Sachin wore his rubber gloves and a head lamp before starting the outline on her skin.

The electric tattoo machine inserts ink into the skin by repeatedly dipping the needles in and out of the surface. When the machine started its first line, the girl reacted as though someone had poked her. I observed each movement of each line very carefully. The direction of the movement was from the bottom to the top. After every line of ink, Sachin wiped the skin with glycerin. While doing the shading of the letters he was super focused on his work. Each time he switched from one colour to another, he cleaned the needles and tips thoroughly.

While doing the tattoo, Sachin told the girl about all the important points for post-care, like not to submerge the tattooed area in water for two weeks. He added that a few people were allergic to the ink, and he was glad that she didn't seem to have this problem. Finally, he coloured in the butterflies, and the whole thing looked very romantic. It had taken an hour to complete that tiny tattoo.

The Tito's lane was bustling till two in the morning. A few more people walked into the shop and asked about the works, but none of them opted for a tattoo.

I enjoyed watching the various characters pop in and out. One was Baba from Nigeria, who used to provide drugs to the firangis coming to the beach. He wore a khaki raincoat, had big headphones wrapped around his head, nearly ten necklaces made of seashells around his neck and a key tied on his right foot. He looked like an alien to me. Manish introduced us and I greeted him. Baba spoke a few words in Hindi, stressing on each syllable.

There was a funny guy, Vinod, who worked as a tour guide. He knew every long-staying firangi in the area. His Hindi accent was mixed with Konkani and had a bit of a fluctuating pitch. Whenever he visited the studio he would say something that made everyone laugh. A group of guys and girls were posing for photographs in front of our studio and his observation was quite hilarious: '*Aajkal kaun kiska girlfriend hai kisko pata hai re baba. Kaun kiske saath chipak raha hai*!'

Our studio didn't have a lavatory, so whenever I needed to go to the toilet, I had to go to the one near the beach. On my way I bumped into the cannabis dealers and pimps who operated there. In the course of the week I met a whole lot of characters.

It was early morning by the time we closed the studio. We headed to the house Sachin and Manish had rented. Manish told me there was no problem in parking the bike on the street next to the house. The very creatively messy room had a few paintings including a striking portrait of a man. I asked Sachin who it was, and he showed me his calf. There was a tattoo of the same portrait inked on it. It turned out that Sachin was a big fan of Spanish painter Salvador Dali, the famous surrealist. The portrait and tattoo were created to inspire him.

*

I didn't want to waste my whole day sleeping, so instead I set off to check out a few places. A few of my friends were studying at the Goa Institute of Management which was towards the Sanquelium side. Once I reached Mapusa, I asked someone for directions. It was raining lightly, and driving through the green landscape of Goa was an awesome feeling. On the way, I stopped for tea and a pancake.

By the time I reached Bicholim the downpour was so heavy that I had to look for shelter. It felt like the rain could rip through the bike's petrol tank. I was looking for a tree under which I could shelter for a while. I finally found a huge banyan tree and stood under it for almost twenty minutes but there was no sign of the rain stopping. I was drenched from the water that fell from the leaves.

Finally, I resumed my journey. Once I reached the Goa Institute of Management, I called my friends Hardik and Subhasis, and they took me around the beautiful campus. I missed my student days; something that always happened to me when I entered a beautifully designed educational institution.

On the way back to the studio I bought an orange to practice tattooing. It was very difficult to keep the machine steady while drawing the dots and lines.

*

Back at the studio, Manish showed me some fake skins he had practiced tattooing on in his early days. I realized it would take at least a month to get a hang of the nuances of tattooing.

The next day was Monday, and as Sachin said, there weren't many people walking through our lane. Those who entered our studio just went through the tattoo albums and asked about the prices.

'Hi Andy,' Sachin greeted a firangi who had entered our studio late in the afternoon. Andy was a backpacker from Australia who had been in Goa for the last three months. He had fallen in love with India and wanted to take something back as a memory. Sachin had done a coloured tattoo of a peacock feather down his back. The idea behind the peacock feather came about for two reasons. By a happy coincidence, the peacock is the national bird of India, the country he loves, and his girlfriend's last name was also Peacock. He planned to surprise her with the tattoo when he returned.

He had been so impressed by the work that he began popping into the studio nearly every evening. Sachin told him to show me his tattoo. It was beautiful, a true work of art.

Andy had lost his father to cancer. He wanted a big, full sleeve tattoo to pay tribute to him, but he was confused about the design. Andy's father's name was Jack and he was well-known in their locality. Andy recalled how his father used to read him stories as a kid. His favourite story was *Jack and the Beanstalk*. His idea for the tattoo was a beanstalk going up along his arm, leading to a palace in the clouds where his dad would be chilling out.

Sachin took up the challenge and started working on paper to give shape to the idea. He drew a sketch and Andy added more to it. His dad had loved to fish so he added a fishing line and hook dangling from the clouds, to where a giant koi fish was swimming. The fish represented his mother, who is from Japan. After that he added two of his pet dogs, one hiding inside the beanstalk and the other looking out from behind it. Once the whole design was done on paper, it looked incredible.

Now it was time to ink the design on skin. The problem was that Andy was going to leave in three days, so there wasn't much time to get a full sleeve done. Sachin said that such a piece needed at least a week of sittings but he could complete it in two stretches of long sessions, fifteen hours each.

When the tattooing began, we devoted two days to it, literally. We didn't leave the studio except to go to the bathroom. We had a lot of Red Bull, and in the background Andy was playing his dad's favourite music on repeat.

My perception of tattooing changed. I had thought of tattoos as small works of art which take at most a few hours. I had no idea that some people love far more elaborate designs that could go on for days. Sachin managed to pull it off in two days. It was well worth it. The design stole Andy's heart.

Over that week, I fell in love with Goa's monsoon, its dishes, freshly caught seafood, King's beer, the conversations with people popping in and out of the studio, especially Baba and Vinod, and even the inebriated crowd in the lane. I had made a few good friends as well.

One evening, as I was leaving the beach and heading towards the studio, I was approached by a pimp. '*Saab kuch chahiye kya?*' He was asking if I wanted the whole package. I wanted to have some fun so I continued the conversation. I asked '*Kya?*'

He probably thought that I didn't understand his tempting offer so he spelt it out. 'Goa is a happening place where people come to enjoy themselves. Do you need anything for the entertainment?'

'Entertainment? Meaning…?' I asked.

'People go to nightclubs with girls,' he said.

'That I know, but what entertainment are you talking about?' I asked again.

He must have thought I hadn't caught on so he spelt it out. 'Do you want a girl?'

Someone patted my back and I spun around. 'Hey dude, what's happening?' It was Baba, the Nigerian drug dealer. He introduced me to the pimp and said that I worked in the tattoo studio. The pimp looked embarrassed.

'But you didn't tell me how much it costs!' I said to him as he was leaving.

There was a fish therapy shop next to our studio. It was quite popular with girls. More of a salon, they offered pedicures of a different kind. Customers would put their feet in a large water tank and the fish inside would nibble away at the dead skin.

I glanced inside with the hope of seeing Janessa. And there she was, sitting on a bench with her feet in the water tank! She wore a blue wrap-around skirt and a pink tanktop. Her curly blonde hair covered half her face. I entered the shop instinctively but seeing her up close I froze and was tongue-tied for a moment.

I managed to say, 'Hey! Look, I found you!' She laughed and said 'No, I found you!' She had seen from my Facebook profile that I was at Inkbaba. I smiled at her. 'It's so good to see you,' I said. 'Me too,' she said.

Sachin raised his eyebrows when Janessa and I entered the studio. 'Janessa, right?' he asked. Janessa gave me a quizzical look. I just smiled but didn't say anything.

She sat down on the bean bag and I took a chair next to

her. After Andy's long tattooing session we were all feeling a bit low as there had been no big projects since then. All of us were missing him and we spoke very little. Janessa brought fresh energy into the studio. She started talking to Manish and Sachin about tattooing and cracked jokes, making the ambience lively. Sachin asked her if she had a tattoo yet. She replied with a beautiful line: 'Art is just a visible form of repressed feelings. I don't believe in repressing feelings.'

As Janessa went through the tattoo album she stared at one particular design for a long time. Sachin asked if she wanted that design. She wasn't sure but if she wanted a tattoo it would be that one. It was of a dangerous cobra with an intimidating widespread hood.

Sachin explained that the cobra tattoo is regarded as a symbol of sovereign power and wisdom. In Indian mythology, Nagas guard the great treasure in an abandoned temple, so the cobra is regarded as a protector of great treasures.

Janessa told him about our snake encounter in Himachal. She had conquered her fear of reptiles in India, and she wanted to take that memory back with her.

'You've been working here for a week. Have you done a tattoo yet?' I showed her the few tattooed oranges I had been practising on. She looked amused. I clarified that my boss didn't want me to ruin anyone's skin with my experiments. She tied up her hair with a band and said I could do a tattoo on the back of her neck. 'You can ruin it,' she said. I was bit nervous as well as secretly thrilled by her trust in me.

Sachin was trying to give me confidence, saying that he would guide me while I worked. I knew that no matter how careful I was while operating the machine, there would be some amount of pain. Moreover, I would be tattooing someone I liked, and this worried me more. Janessa punched my chest. 'Come on, you always think too much,' she said.

I sprung up to fetch the tattoo machine. We had a flash art of a cobra hood so it wasn't difficult to do the outline. Sachin directed me to place the tattoo below the collar bone; the more fleshy the area, he said, the less painful it would be. We played some music to distract Janessa from the pain. I had not been that cautious while practising on the orange but now I took great care while injecting the ink into Janessa. The shading part of the cobra hood wasn't perfect but Sachin said he would give it a finishing touch. Janessa refused. She said she wanted the tattoo just the way I had done it.

*

Much later Janessa and I set out for a walk from Baga towards Calangute. It was midnight and the beach was deserted. The lapping sounds of waves and the cool breeze made us feel relaxed.

It started drizzling so we sheltered in a little hut made out of coconut leaves. Janessa sat down on the sand, hugging her knees, lit a cigarette and handed one to me. I was playing with a handful of sand, running it through my fingers. Janessa asked whether we should go towards the water. I said no as she had just got a tattoo done and the sea water could fuel an infection.

We sat there in silence for some time then Jessica said, 'You know, you are the first Indian friend I have made.' I put my arm around her, remembering our time in Himachal. She put her arm around my waist and turned to face me. 'What did you think when I decided to have the tattoo?' I said, in a very low tone, 'Like you said, art is just a visible form of repressed feelings. I think this one brought us closer.'

She was silent for a long moment then she said, 'Though I do embrace sexual liberation, let me tell you one thing very straight: I like you.' I liked her openness, the matter-of-fact way she spoke. I wished I could be like her. 'I like you too,' I said.

She had tilted her chin up and we kissed lightly. She looked away from me for some time. 'You know what, you talk to people, you laugh with people, you get close to people, but some part of you is closed off from everyone. You are looking for someone to pop out of the sea and hug you tightly.'

I had not told her about Sameen. People say that the intensity of a relationship declines with time, but that was not the case for me, not then. One woman had stolen my heart, and I had not been open to a relationship since then. I was filled with memories of Sameen, the most beautiful woman I had ever met. When I stayed silent, Janessa realized that her earlier observation had been spot-on. 'What's her name?'

I told her about Sameen and my unrequited love. How I had met her when she had already found someone; the reason why I could not express my feelings, my orthodox family, the religious divide.

'So you didn't even let her know how you felt?' I nodded. She said, 'Don't repress your feelings. This will destroy you from the inside. Just call her and tell her.' I clarified that I hadn't been in touch with her. She had changed her number and did not have any online presence. It had been six years since we had last spoken.

We had a long discussion during which she tried to convince me that I should express my feelings to Sameen. I tried to convince her that I was fine and had accepted the reality. She concluded the conversation with her opinion, which was that I wasn't over Sameen as yet.

We spent the night in the hut. Early the next morning, Janessa woke me up and said she wanted to take me somewhere. I didn't know where we were heading but I just followed her directions.

We parked the bike and climbed a hill scattered with loose pebbles and stones. At first sight it looked like a fort. As we entered through a rocky entrance, there was a large area covered with grass and rocks. We walked further towards the ruins of the rock walls and climbed onto them. From there, the view of the Arabian Sea was stunning.

We sat there for hours, holding hands and looking at the sea. We might have sat there the whole day if no one had come by and disturbed the serenity. It was my last day in Goa, and we both wanted to spend time together. We visited all the popular beaches, and travelled into the countryside. We went to the beautiful Basilica of Bom Jesus Church, where the body of Francis Xavier has been kept since 1552. Janessa told me that some local people believed that the nails of the body were still growing.

After travelling the whole day, we went to the place where

Janessa was staying. She had a bottle of the local cashew feni, and we both had a glass. By then it was evening, time for me to head back to the tattoo studio. We were both rather quiet, not sure when we would meet again as her month in India was almost up. She knew I was headed south. She wouldn't be coming to Tito's with me. We hugged for a long time as we said goodbye. I felt like I was losing a good friend again.

10. Karnataka

Assisting an Emotion Management Counsellor

Bangalore had changed a lot in the six years I had been away. I had lived in the city for six months after the completion of my engineering degree.

Many of my friends had been offered jobs through campus placements well before they passed out, but I was jobless at that point of time. The reason for this was that I had never been able to go through puzzle books, mugging up vocabulary and quantitative math to get into a software engineering job. I was quite good at computer programming, which would have been my primary job as a software engineer, but unfortunately, that was not the first criterion to get into the software world. I was always rejected at the first step, the written test, before I had a chance to show my technical skills.

I borrowed some money from my father and moved to Bangalore, assuring my parents that I would get a job before the money ran out. Getting a job took me six months. During that time, I was staying with my senior, Shakti bhai. He was a technical geek and always inspired me to do my level best to get through the interviews.

By then Bangalore was already known as the IT city

of India, and rightly so. But there were dark sides to the employment sector because of some unscrupulous set-ups that were out to exploit the market. I got to know this side of the job market; of how some consultancies trapped freshers who were willing to do anything to get placed.

One of my experiences was with a consultancy that took money from me upfront and then called me for a job interview. They lectured me on my English accent. After fifteen days and three interviews with the same consultancy, I got to know that it was for a call centre job, although I had applied for a software job. Those were the kind of frauds they perpetuated.

I came to know of a recruitment drive for Tata Consultancy Services. There must have been a huge number of applicants and thousands of candidates appeared for the interview. My preparation went well and I cleared the written test. I had cleared three levels of certifications in the Oracle database development track and was OCP-certified before joining TCS. The interviewer was very impressed with the OCP logo on my resume and selected me without asking too many questions. I soon moved to Trivandrum to get training for my first job.

*

After I had a job lined up in Bangalore for my project, I got in touch with Shakti bhai to let him know I would be in town. He told me that he was a married bachelor as his wife was away on work for a month. He insisted that I stay at his place.

My Facebook status for my week in Bangalore read: I am working as an emotion management consultant for a week. Anyone who is dissatisfied with their job, confused about their career path, befuddled about how to discover their passion or in any kind of confusion related to work, please do write in to my ID to meet me and discuss.

'Job Satisfaction' was at the crux of my mission's objective: 'to discover your passion'.

Whenever an issue like job satisfaction is raised in big corporate circles, people dig out points like HR policy, workplace environment, salary hike, employee retention rate, working hours, manager subordinate relationship, employee recognition, etc. But no one wants to go back to the basics. Invariably, the root cause for dissatisfaction is when someone sacrifices their dreams and chooses a track they had never wanted to be in. This gives rise to negative emotions like frustration, irritation, anger and unhappiness.

The counsellor who had helped me secure this job was an expert in emotion management. He told me that it would not be possible to do this job properly in one week. So my role would be to interact with people, collect information from them and give it to him. He handed me a questionnaire to be used.

I woke up to a pleasant morning, so typical of Bangalore, and started my day with a cup of coffee. I was really excited as well nervous about the day, as I would be interacting with people facing real issues. The excitement didn't end, even when I closed the door of my soundproof cabin at the office.

There was a knock on the door and a man entered. When

I saw his unshaven, pale face, I got frightened. I got up from the chair and said 'Hello. Please take a seat.' Unlike in most of my earlier jobs where I had had some idea of what my duties entailed, here I was learning on the go.

I handed him a form that required his basics. He was from Andhra Pradesh, and his name was Arun. He had been working as a software engineer for the last five years. He had been married for a year. His wife was working in an IT firm in Chennai. He had dark circles around his eyes, pointing to a sleeping disorder. When I told him about my earlier IT experiences, he looked more at ease. In our thirty-minute conversation, Arun began to unveil, layer by layer, his problems of anxiety. I took notes as he spoke. I told him to imagine that there was nobody in the room besides him and to travel through his life over the last ten years. I persuaded him not to filter his thoughts and tell me whatever came to his mind.

Arun had been born in a middle-class family. Until his intermediate, he didn't face any problems with guidance; like everyone around him, he pursued science after getting a first class in matriculation. But he was confused about what to do after that. Some of his cousins had done engineering, and encouraged him to do the same since there was scope to earn a lot of money in IT. As they said, 25,000 rupees per month was a big amount for a middle-class guy. Arun had been playing cricket but his father had broken his cricket bat just before the intermediate exam. After that he never played cricket again.

When he landed up in engineering, he was happy to have

made good friends. Around that time he fell in love for the first time but didn't dare to say anything to the girl till the end of fourth year. He developed a hobby of painting in his fourth year as well. In the last semester, he made a beautiful painting of his beloved and presented it to her. She was very touched and also realized that it was his way of telling her that he was in love with her. Soon she too reciprocated. They grew closer over the year and all was well till she told her parents about it. Like many Indian love stories, here too caste became an obstacle and the girl's parents arranged her marriage to someone else. His story was almost like mine!

Arun took up a job in Bangalore. He didn't want to get married and made excuses for three years, till his mother created some emotional drama at home. Finally, he was married to a girl in the same field. The problem was that she was working in Chennai. At first they had thought that she would get a transfer to Bangalore, but she had still not managed to do so.

Arun's project manager had assured him of an assignment abroad, so he bought a house. Most of his salary was going towards the home loan. He had been hoping to earn in dollars for two years and pay off the loan, but when his project got cancelled it put him in a tight spot financially.

He was assigned to a production support job, and instead of enjoying married life, he was working on night shifts. 'I can't sleep. Even when I doze off there's no sense of being asleep. I feel lethargic all day. I don't feel like working, eating nor doing anything, and I have mood swings. Sometimes I feel like life is worthless.'

I felt sorry for him but couldn't find the words to console him. I suggested that he should make a plan and put it down on paper, listing all the things he wanted to do or achieve in life. Against each point I told him to write down how things would turn positive once he had achieved that goal. I also told him to list all the things that would turn negative if he were not able to achieve his goals. I wrote down my points and observations before sending him to my boss. I tried to console him by saying that everything would be fine, that it was just a temporary bad phase of life.

Cities may look smart with their big towers and glass structures but many people face all kinds of problems. I met people with professional issues ranging from bad rapport with their managers, to not getting recognition commensurate with their performance, from communal politics in the office to offshore work distribution, onsite politics to reallocation issues. Some complained of feeling worthless when they were not able to perform as well as their peers. In some cases, problems arose when couples were assigned to different locations. Getting leave during pregnancy seemed to be an issue. I was stunned when a woman told me that when her brother died in an accident and she asked for a transfer back home, the reallocation unit asked for an autopsy report. I couldn't believe the insensitivity.

Many of my Bangalore friends had faced back issues due to sitting in one position for hours. I myself felt heavy after listening to all those issues over the week. The IT industry itself seemed to have stagnated over the last few years. Previously, the onsite to offshore ratio had been higher and many people got the opportunity to go abroad and earn in dollars. Now the ratio had been drastically reduced because the billing was not that high for onsite people, so companies tried to do most of their work in India. Visas too had become more difficult.

*

Marathalli in Bengaluru is a locality popular with Odias. I was happy to see that the neighbourhood still had the same bakery shop. It was crowded as usual with people ordering its popular ready-to-eat items like buns, pao, patties and rolls. The liquor shop was in the same spot. I bought a bottle of Old Monk rum to share with Shakti bhai on my last evening. Back at Shakti's home, I cooked Odia dalma and chicken kasa with rice.

During my earlier time in Bangalore we had to chase water tankers on weekend mornings and store it for a week. Water used to be a major problem. Shakti bhai and I reminisced over this and many other things.

He recalled one of our visits to the Chennai Crocodile Park, and the photo of him holding a crocodile with his hand. This gave me the idea of volunteering there but I knew no one who could connect me to the place. I was off to Chennai next, hopeful and confident that I would be able to do some *jugaad* to get a job there.

11. Tamil Nadu

Selling Peanuts on Marina Beach

I had plenty of beautiful memories of Chennai. As the saying goes, one cannot forget one's first job and first love, and this city had given me both. After my initial training period in Trivandrum, I was posted to the Chennai branch of TCS. Here I met my love, Sameen, the woman I still hadn't gotten over. The climate of this city, the fragrance of the breeze, the sight of the beaches, early morning buses, all these made me feel nostalgic. I was overcome with memories of her as I passed the familiar streets. When my bus crossed the Adyar Bridge, I couldn't hold back my tears. It had been six long years but my feelings for her were as fresh as ever.

I remembered the first time Sameen and I had gone to Besant Nagar beach. Our conversation took us to a different level. I remembered sitting on the sand, talking to her over many weekends. Everywhere I looked, I saw her image; the surroundings brought back vivid images. I could smell the perfume she used to wear.

I was the only one to get down at Thiruvanmiyur, the last stop on this route. This was where I had been staying when Sameen left Chennai. The best part of this week was that I was going to stay at my best friend's house. Shibashis and I had been friends since our engineering days. We had shared every small thing that happened in our lives.

Shibashis had had rented a house near his office, Siruseri IT Park. I had to take another local bus towards Padur to reach his place. The good thing about his house was that the crocodile park was not very far.

Shibashis was ready to leave for work by the time I arrived. I greeted him with 'Ready ready!' It had been his catchphrase in college. His wife had gone to Odisha to take an exam, so Shibashis was a married bachelor for the week.

I took a bus towards Kelambakam and then towards the crocodile park, which is on the road to Mahabalipuram. The park was nearly forty years old. It is a reptile zoo and research centre founded by Romulus Whitaker. I am a big fan of his passion for the conservation of endangered species.

The last time I had been there with Shakti bhai, I had been frightened on seeing thousands of crocodiles in one place. But slowly, I became fascinated with the zoo. It had started with just 30 mugger adults. The successful breeding programme took the numbers to thousands. I really wanted to experience working at the zoo.

At the ticket counter, I asked to meet the office staff. After ten minutes of persuasion, the staffer allowed me to go inside to the research area. I spoke with the concerned person but unfortunately volunteering to work there required going through a lengthy process, and could only be done after a few weeks. I regretted not having contacted them earlier.

I approached various GRE coaching institutes, looking to

see if they could take me on for a week to teach vocabulary. Basically I intended to utilize my mugging of thirty-five hundred words for my own GRE preparation. But these institutes refused to employ me for just a week; they were sceptical about how it would help them.

I was clueless and jobless and took a bus towards Marina Beach to think it over and find a solution. It was strange that I was jobless in the state where I had started my career.

*

Marina Beach is the heart of Chennai. I have a lot of memories connected with this place. I visited it for the first time with my parents and sister. I remember my mother bought a garland made of jasmine flowers and wound it in her hair, inspired by the Tamilian women on the beach. My sister took a picture to freeze that memory.

The first time I went to Marina Beach with Sameen, I wanted to surprise her and take her to the aquarium nearby but it was closed that particular day. We met at Marina Beach every Sunday after that.

I could recall our last conversation before Sameen left Chennai. It was a moment that hovered between togetherness and separation, a relationship that was still hanging between friendship and love. She was sitting next to me, writing our names on the sand, murmuring the song *Jaane kya dhoondta hai, yeh mera dil, Tujhko kya chaahiye zindagi.*

I was all right with my new job, and not expecting much from life. We had a brief chat about our lives that ended with an abrupt silence. She was the one who broke the silence saying, 'I want you to make a name for yourself.' They were the most encouraging words I had ever heard, words that kept me chasing my dreams.

Whenever I felt lonely after Sameen left I would come down to this crowded beach. I enjoyed watching the madness of the waves, the golden sands, the sky changing with the sunset, the ships in the distance, the lovers behind the discarded boats, and obviously the food sellers.

I had some fish fry and again started walking down the beach, away from the crowd. The further I walked, the less littered the beach was. I was looking at two small kids playing with kites in the distance.

A little while later a young boy selling peanuts came towards me. He looked barely eight. He was struggling to walk while carrying a heavy basket of peanuts and roasted chickpeas. He asked me whether I wanted some of his sundal. I bought a pack for ten rupees.

The child must have been tired of carrying the bamboo basket. He sat down and asked, 'Why you sit here?' One good thing about Chennai is that even the common man can communicate in broken English. When I asked he said that his mother worked as a housemaid, and the lady of the house taught him English sometimes. The smart kid practiced his English with tourists and others on Marina Beach. Selvam had dropped out of school after his father died in order to help his mother with some additional money.

By the time I got back it was late in the evening. Shibashis had returned from the office. We had a drink and spoke about various things but I was still thinking about that little sundal seller. I could not sleep that night. I was still jobless. I wondered if I could help Selvam, maybe by holding his heavy basket and helping to sell peanuts around the beach. It would be a job that would kill my corporate ego, and a totally new experience.

I went back to Marina Beach the next day. Being a weekday, it wasn't as crowded. Finally, Selvam appeared late in the afternoon. I told him about my interest in helping him by holding his basket. At first he was hesitant and would not accept my help. When I said that I wanted to help him like he wanted to help his mother, he gave me the basket.

We started walking down the beach yelling 'Sundal! Sundal!' A lot of people gave us weird looks, but the sight of this odd pair drew others to buy. The beach got quite crowded by the evening and our basket was empty. Selvam was very happy and agreed to meeting the next day.

The whole week was fun. I really enjoyed the awestruck looks we got as we walked down the beach selling peanuts. Selvam began to open up to me. He made jokes about how people were staring at us, and suggested that I not wear my glasses. According to him, they made me look even less like a peanut seller. I tried to behave the way my little boss told me to, but didn't feel comfortable without my glasses.

One day, Selvam introduced me to his mother, and translated our exchange. She was worried about his not going to school. I tried to persuade him but he was adamant. He reminded me of the protagonist in *Slumdog Millionaire*, refusing to be held back by his circumstances. He told me he had dreams of opening a restaurant on the beach someday.

On Saturday, the beach was packed. It looked like all the office-goers had come out to enjoy the breeze. Our sales were good that day, which meant we didn't have to walk very far along the beach. Among the crowd, I thought I saw a vaguely familiar face, someone who looked like my ex-colleague Bhawani. It was her and another old colleague, Vishnu. They asked for two packets. They hadn't recognized me, perhaps because of my long hair and shabby get-up. I didn't reveal my identity just then.

After they walked away I scrolled down the contacts on my phone and found Bhawani's number. I called her and told her to walk back to the place where she had just bought sundal. When they came back, Bhawani was curious and asked me why and what I was doing. I told them about my project and they shared that they had just got married.

I knew a bit about Vishnu. It was no different from that of many other Indian-origin Tamils in Sri Lanka who had fled to India during the civil war.

Their forefathers were migrant labour taken to the island by the British to work in the tea plantations. All was okay till independence. Under an agreement between the two countries' governments in the 1960s, around 40 per cent of the Tamils were granted Sri Lankan nationality. Many of the rest were sent to India between 1970 and 1980 and were given Indian citizenship. Ethnic conflicts have existed since then.

Once the dispute started between Sri Lankan Tamils and the Sinhalese people, the game of politics made the situation bitter which led to the civil war. As always, history repeated itself, and the first casualties were innocent civilians. While I was thinking about Vishnu and his story, it had started raining and people were leaving. We had made good sales and our basket was almost empty. I calculated the day's earnings and handed the money to Selvam. I advised him to join a school but he was adamant. He flashed a wide smile as always, and we said goodbye.

As I started walking towards the nearest bus stand, I thought I saw Sameen running towards the beach with a man. There was a green scarf wrapped around her head, which made her look more beautiful. Perhaps meeting Bhawani had stirred up memories. I thought that I had really seen Sameen but realized it was all in my imagination.

12. Kerala

Steering a Houseboat Through the Backwaters

As I got on a night bus from Chennai to Alleppey, I was looking forward to being in the backwaters of Kerala. From the very beginning of my journey, I had been hoping for this as being on a houseboat was something I really wanted to experience. Thanks to my Malayali friend Adarsh, I would work as an assistant to a houseboat captain. The jetty at Alleppey is the place for houseboats and ferries to set sail. I was lucky to be there in August. The second Saturday of the month is when the annual snake boat races are held. As I went down the road to the jetty, I could see hundreds of houseboats anchored near the Punnamada Lake. Some of them were beautifully decorated.

I called up the captain I would be serving under, and he guided me towards our boat. It was anchored far away from the shore, so we had to hop from one boat to another to reach it. While stepping onto the boat, the captain told me that I had come at the wrong time. It was the off-season, and very few tourists came to Kerala during the monsoon. Most of the houseboats were anchored here because they were not getting enough visitors. Even we had only two trips booked for that week. The captain left the houseboat after introducing me to everyone. There was a cook, a helper and a pilot, whose name was Hari. Luckily for me, he could speak good English.

At the centre of the boat there was a big deck where we sat to chat. Hari told me that the boat had been booked for Wednesday and Friday, and on the rest of the days it would be anchored here. I was told that I would get a lot of time to roam around Alleppey. He showed me around the houseboat, which had two fully furnished AC bedrooms, one open lounge, a kitchen, and a small room for the staff. I put my luggage there. A walkway connected the rooms, and safety equipment like jackets and lifebuoys hung on the walls.

I went back to shore to have breakfast at a street-food joint. Everyone seemed to be eating rice, so I nodded when the waiter asked. He placed a glass of pink liquid on the table. It was chukkuvellam, which is boiled water with a blend of herbs. I drank it, thinking the hot water could help clear my stomach. The waiter brought a plate of rice topped with a big piece of fish. When I asked whether there was any vegetarian curry available, he just took the fish off the rice!

What a coincidence! My experience in the northern-most state and southern-most state shared similarities: water and boats! In Jammu & Kashmir I had spent my time white-water rafting and here I had chosen work on a houseboat. One runs on the turbulent white water, another on the serene, stagnant blue-back water.

I was very excited as on my first day our group arrived and we would be setting off soon. The passengers were two recently married couples. They were visibly excited when they stepped on board. Each couple walked through the whole boat with exhilaration before checking into their respective rooms.

The greatest joy was when we reached a point where we were the only ones in the middle of the backwaters. That was when Hari showed me how to handle the steering. After observing for half an hour, I got a chance to operate it. I was more than thrilled, feeling almost like the pilot of a giant cruise ship.

Our passengers had freshened up and joined us on deck. After my week in Goa, I had been missing the chit-chat of travellers, and so made the most of it.

While having lunch, Hari invited me to dinner at his home. Our boat would be anchored at his village for the night. The boat stopped in front of Hari's home at six in the evening. His daughter ran towards the boat and Hari gave her a radiant smile. The sunset made the whole setting even more beautiful and I immediately clicked the moment. I took a long walk through the village, enjoying the paddy fields, chatting with people who spoke some broken English, and tried my hand at fishing before going back to Hari's home. I had a nice Kerala dinner, including a few sips of the local toddy.

Back on deck, I sat like the Buddha for nearly the whole night, gazing at the stars. For some reason, I was thinking a lot about Sameen.

The next morning, the boat resumed the journey. We sailed through the rippling backwaters and headed back to the jetty. While we refuelled, Hari told me about the history of the modern houseboat, and that the industry had begun just thirty years ago, in the early 1990s. Earlier, boats with a canopy (usually called kettuvallam or rice boats) had been used to transport grains from the isolated villages of Kerala to the towns. With the advent of land transport facilities, the rice boats went off the scene. Around that time, a German man had observed that these rice boats usually accommodated a driver and a cook for long stays. If they could stay, then why couldn't tourists? And thus began a new industry.

Hari complained about the low salary, and said that their houseboat workers' union had gone on a long strike a few months earlier. The salary of an experienced pilot and a new one were the same. This was the product of communist policies.

On Thursday I didn't have much to do other than spend time with my co-workers, playing cards, listening to their stories, roaming around Alleppey's beaches, and walking across the backwater rivulet. Hari had become a good friend. He was a man with many stories, and had experienced many things in life. Talking to him gave me a different perspective on the wages of Indian workers in Dubai. He had spent some time there, working as a cab driver.

Our next trip would be from Alappuzha (Alleppey) to Kottayam. I was told that this was one of the most exotic, breathtaking backwater channels in the state. Before the tourists arrived, the cook rushed to the kitchen to prepare tea to welcome them. Hari and I were on deck, chatting with the boat owner, a cool guy who told me that I should have come during the peak season to experience the tourist rush.

Sometimes the same houseboat's prices could go up to ten times more during late December.

A young married couple approached our boat. My eyes widened. I couldn't believe who it was! I felt as though my heart had flipped over.

She looked a bit different, more mature, more beautiful, more elegant, but easily recognizable by her graceful walk. A green dupatta was wrapped around her head. It was the lady to whom I had lost my heart, the lady I had lost hope of meeting again, the lady who with one look, could make me turn a somersault in the middle of a crowd. It was Sameen!

I guessed that the man she was with was her husband. I smiled when she climbed aboard, but Sameen behaved as if she didn't know me. She and her husband proceeded towards their room. I was more than a bit upset. Hari sensed that something had happened when I had seen her. He asked me about it but I was evasive. Our boat embarked on its journey.

In the evening, Hari suggested we head to the nearest local bar. He tried to persuade me but I refused. I just wanted to sit on deck, gazing at the sky. Suddenly I heard a voice that made my heart pound a thousand times. 'This is why I like you, you know.'

Sameen was standing just a few feet away. I stood up and smiled at her. The sound of her voice was still echoing in the air. Then I broke the silence. 'I thought you didn't recognize me.' She admitted that her husband was possessive of her. When we were in Chennai, she had spoken often of her love and how she couldn't marry anyone but him. 'So, did you marry your love?' I asked her.

For a moment she was silent, and then she said no.

I felt like someone had slapped my face. I hadn't proposed to her because she loved someone else, and now she had married a different guy. I didn't say anything for some time.

I looked at her. She was as beautiful as ever. I had seen many beautiful women in these five years and some of them had caught my eye, but I had never connected with anyone the way I had with her. When I looked at Sameen I realized how she was different from the whole world, how confident and intelligent she was. Throughout my journey I had tried to inspire others, and now my inspiration was standing right next to me.

'Are you okay?' she asked. 'I'm sorry, I got lost in the sky,' I said. She responded in a flirtatious tone. 'Sometimes you are lost with real people.' I replied with a smile, 'You are heaven, everything else is just sky.' She blushed for a moment. 'You know you are flirting with a married woman.'

I realized that Sameen would leave before her husband appeared. I knew time was ticking, and I had to make my feelings known to her, take Janessa's advice before she walked out of my life again.

I didn't want to lose that moment, so I sighed and said, 'I love you Sameen. I loved you the moment I saw you. I repressed my feelings, knowing you loved someone else. Now that we are meeting again, you are married. I am sorry to tell you all this now, but I can't repress my feelings anymore. When you left Chennai, I searched for you for so long. I know it's illogical to say this now, but I just want to tell you there has not been a single day when I haven't thought about you. I love your smile, I love the way you talk, I love your graceful walk, I love everything you do. I will never love anyone but you. I love you with all my heart. Why did you leave Chennai without saying goodbye properly?'

She clasped my hands in hers, and looked as though she were about to speak. At that moment, we heard someone coming on deck. A million expressions seemed to flicker across Sameen's face, but I realized where we were, and the context, when I saw Sameen's husband. They both left and went to their room.

I didn't know whether I had done the right thing in expressing myself. But I felt relaxed, having let go of the things that had been bothering me for years.

13. Andhra Pradesh

Dealing with Toddlers' Tantrums at a Playschool

Meeting Sameen had been the most beautiful thing that had happened to me on this journey, and leaving her was the most painful of all. I lost myself in thoughts of her, only breaking out of it when the train's whistle blew, signalling the departure for Hyderabad.

At first I had planned to go to Vizag to work at a fishery. On the eve of my departure from Alleppey, Telengana was officially sanctioned as the twenty-ninth state of India. It would be carved out of Andhra Pradesh, and Hyderabad would serve as the common administrative capital for both the states for some time. Deciding that the capital would be a better option, I changed my plans.

Many of my college friends were now based in Hyderabad, so accommodation was not going to be an issue. My only worry was finding a job since I had not made arrangements in advance. I started by cold-calling all my friends in Hyderabad, asking if they could find me a job for a week. After thirty rejections, one clicked.

I would be working as a teacher in a playschool for an NGO. Bhumi was an organization that believed in promoting leadership at the grassroots level. It had been associated with many projects seeking to empower people. The founder, Abdul Mujeeb Khan, was a very optimistic person. Once I began telling him about my journey, and myself, he was very positive about the entire thing. He told me about the playgroup division, and I was excited to teach and learn child psychology. I was very happy to experience the education system from the perspective of little kids.

At around nine, kids began queuing for classes, most accompanied by their mothers. The calm and serene environment at once turned into a busy, noisy place. Some kids started crying as soon as their parents left them. I understood that consoling them was my primary task but I had no idea how to do that. The other teachers knew exactly how to lure the kids into the classes. I would have to learn from them.

The entire situation took me back to my schooldays. The only difference was that now I was on the other side of the desk. There were fifteen kids in my classroom, aged between two to four years. The youngest ones were the naughtiest. I felt like they were ragging me. After a lot of trouble, I somehow managed to make all the kids sit, but one kid opened up his tiffin box. His neighbour did the same. They both started eating, sharing food. One of them took out a packet of chips but even after struggling a lot, he couldn't tear it open so he passed the packet to the other one, asking for help. The other smarty poked his steel spoon into the wrapper but he still didn't manage to open it.

Observing them and their innocence gave me extraordinary

pleasure. I let them try their way first and then took the wrapper from them to show them how to open it. Children must be taught to experiment with things and made to find solutions by themselves. That is how the seed of curiosity to learn more is sown.

I gave each of them a sheet of paper to make paper boats. A few kids started scribbling on it. The older ones looked at me and tried to copy the way I was making the boat. I failed to retain their attention because of my inexperience in dealing with so many kids at one time. The other teacher came to my rescue. Having spent so much time with the kids, she understood child psychology far better. She made one child copy what she was doing, slowly, fold by fold, and the other kids followed that one.

When she was done with all the folds, she asked the child sitting near her to pull the rear end of the folded paper. When he did so, he was delighted to see the paper boat taking shape. Soon the entire classroom was cheering this new achievement. They were so excited and engrossed with trying to make their first paper boats that none of them cried for some time. It was both a happy and a poignant moment. A tear of triumph rolled down my cheeks. At that moment I decided that if I ever started a school of my own, I would call it the Paper Boat School.

Two-year-old Umar had just started school. It was his first week. I learnt from the other teachers that he was unable to mix with the others and cried most of the time. Umar was enrolled in my classroom. Every time I saw his sad little face, I tried hard to console him. As I began spending time with him, he got attached to me. He would come to me crying and ask to be taken home.

He tugged my hand and took me to a room where toys were stored. Thinking that he wanted to play, I offered him a few toys. But he refused to play and would not touch a single one. He didn't want to go back to class either. His motive behind going to the toy room was only to come out of the classroom. He would not listen to me when I asked him to go with me to the classroom, nor did he allow me to leave.

When I managed to take him to the class and insisted that he sit down, he ran towards the animal chart hanging on the blue wall near the blackboard. I pointed to some of the animals and asked if he could recognize them. He knew the correct answers but answered while still weeping and rubbing his runny nose with his T-shirt. To make the class more interactive, I asked the other kids to join in the animal game. But no matter what I did, he wouldn't stop crying.

'Momma, momma' he cried all day.

'Momma will come if you write,' I lied. Hearing this, he opened his bag and took out his slate. I wrote the letters A and B on the slate and tried to move his hand over the lines. But nothing would keep him silent for long. This pissed me off but I realized that this is what is expected from the job. Tolerance and patience are the two most important qualities required to deal with any child, especially when you are a playgroup teacher. The same process continued for another one hour. God knows how many times I lied to that innocent child.

On seeing my cell phone he stopped crying for a minute but soon started yelling. 'Momma, phone, momma, phone ...'

'I called your Momma, she will come if you start writing,' I said again.

After some time, he found a chocolate in his pocket and pointed, asking to remove the wrapper. As soon as he finished the chocolate, the noise resumed. This time, however, others joined the chorus.

My last experience at the playschool left me smiling. Umar took me to the shoe rack and asked me to wear my shoes using sign language. He wanted me to drop him home.

Working in a school and spending time with young children taught me a lot of things. Grown-ups often see and take things in ways that make our lives messy. Kids certainly know how to keep things simple and easy.

*

Hyderabad certainly knows how to celebrate special occasions. The holy month of Ramadan had begun and all the glitter in every nook and corner of the streets turned the capital of the Nizams into a bride. My friends planned to take me on a tour of the city. While there were Western influences in one small part of Hyderabad, the rest of the city was still steeped in age-old customs.

We went to Hussain Sagar Lake and while on the motor boat, the strong breeze blew away my favourite golf cap. When I told the boatman, he took a dramatic turn to fetch it in the way it is done in action movies. But it was gone and searching for it was a futile exercise. Losing the cap saddened me a bit as I had had it for a long time and it carried a million memories. Little things sometimes have great emotional value.

The Charminar area of Hyderabad was one I had to visit both for its famous landmark monument and its eating places. It was eight and the hustle and bustle of the evening had just started. A tempting aroma filled the air and tickled my taste buds. When I asked around I was directed to a place where more than a hundred people were waiting in a queue to be served haleem, a dish which I'd heard a lot about. The caterer told me that it was especially prepared during the month of Ramadan.

Haleem dates back to the time of the Nizams. The Nizams, it is said, were very selective about the foods they were served. To create a variety of tastes, they spent a lot hiring cooks, some of whom came all the way from the Middle East. The cooks brought along recipes from these other lands. That is how haleem travelled to India, along with a rice dish that added on local flavours to become what is known as the famous Hyderabadi biryani.

Haleem is a stew made of lentils, nuts, minced lamb meat and pounded wheat and usually eaten with naan or rice. It is a delicacy prepared in particular during iftaar, the meal after sunset to break the daily fast during the month of Ramadan. In the restaurants and hotels of old Hyderabad days are devoted to cooking this exotic dish. Hyderabadi haleem is so famous that the dish is exported to other parts of the country and abroad as well. Needless to say, the taste is awesome.

The old part of Hyderabad is filled with tiny shops selling beautiful bangles and attars with different scents. The streets were decorated with colourful lanterns and fireworks lit up the sky. Everybody in Hyderabad was celebrating. I walked down the busy lanes, experiencing the amazing artwork of the bangle industry and beautiful pearls, and felt fortunate to be in Hyderabad at such a festive time.

14. Odisha

Spending a Week in My Own State—Far From Home

Spending a week in one's home state and not meeting one's parents is very frustrating. I had planned on going home but it wasn't working out. Sonepur is some 350 kilometres from Bhubaneswar. Being so close to my home, I had an urge to get off the train and change tracks but I knew I had to control it.

My mother had called to ask whether I would be coming home during the week. She was furious that it wouldn't be happening. Major emotional drama followed but there was nothing I could do as there just wasn't time. That night, my mind was filled with childhood memories. I grew up in a locality that had a lot of kids my age. My sister was just one year older, so we had many common friends. That's probably why Sikan had been more of a friend than a sister.

Our father was against our watching movies. I remembered how we fooled him by showing him the opening sequence of a Hindi film. It featured a one-minute prayer, and he was reassured that it was a good film. What he didn't know was that back then most of the movies would start with a Ganesha Aarti.

Those were the days of tape recorders and father would

bring home cassettes of bhajans. During our adolescent years my sister and I would record over them. One time, when my father thought he had put in a Jagannath bhajan cassette, what he heard instead was the beautiful song *Kaho naa pyaar hai* from the Bollywood film!

I remembered the time when my father bought us a bicycle. Sikan and I took great pride in cleaning it. We never let a spot spoil its beauty.

My father loves gardening. He had planted a few fruit trees in our garden and we loved playing hide and seek among them. Our prized possession was a pomegranate tree. Whenever we found a ripe pomegranate, we would sit down to eat it together with great enthusiasm, but I would always pass Sikan only a handful of the seeds while I ate the rest. Like most siblings, our favourite pastime was bullying each other. However most of the time I was the one behind all the mischief.

I had not seen my family for quite some time and I was missing my sister the most. It may have been because the rest of the country was celebrating Raksha Bandhan, while I was sitting with a bare wrist on a train. I recalled how my sister would fasten the thread in a hurry, more interested in checking out her gift.

Although I had been away from home for quite a few years, my attachment was as strong as ever. Being in my home state after months and still not being able to meet family was very painful.

For my week in Odisha, I had chosen a job in which I could utilize my communication management skills. This week, I was going to work as a TRP analyst at the news channel Kanak TV. It was part of Eastern Media Ltd, one of the biggest media conglomerates in the state. I had been associated with them earlier while working on a Jatra project for a marketing job. This was the only organization about which I had a brief idea before joining.

During my MICA days, we had studied media research. This included learning how different programmes on a channel are positioned and their television rating points or TRPs. I smiled to myself, thinking that those lessons were finally going to be utilized.

Early the next morning, I set off for my new office with enthusiasm. As I reached the main road to get an auto, I was happy to see an aludam-dahibara seller. Two big pots were suspended from each of his bicycle's handlebars. They contained dahi vada and aludam (a spicy potato curry), among the most popular snacks in Bhubaneswar.

As I walked towards him the seller rolled up his sleeves. He squeezed the liquid out of a few vadas, put it on a leaf plate, and topped it with the spicy aludam that made it look colourful and appetising. I told him not to put too much of the powdered spices that are added last as a garnish. *'Bhaina, kam raaga kariba.'* He gave me a wide smile, hearing my local Odia accent. Then he passed me a toothpick, the standard implement instead of forks.

How much I had missed these local foods of Odisha! The street food culture of Bhubaneswar can beat that of any other city in India. In the evening, vendors roam around with many more varieties of snacks. I planned to eat all of them during my week there.

Soon I was on my way to the Eastern Media office. I was familiar with its layout. The ground floor housed the printing division of *Sambad*. Here the air was full of fresh newsprint. Everyone was removing their shoes before going inside, so I did too.

I took the lift to the second floor to reach the news channel division. The security guard asked me whom I wanted to meet and told me to wait at the reception. I recognized some four or five people among those who walked by, all faces I had seen on TV.

Ten minutes later I met the guy who was handling the TRP unit. He pointed out the major divisions of the media channel while we passed through the cabins and reached our cubicle.

Manas appeared to be in his mid-forties. He led me to a desk and handed me a few Excel sheets from which to analyse the TRPs of all the channels available in Odisha. The data he had given me wasn't available except by paid subscription. To get the data, media channels subscribed to it from a company called TAM. This is the same company that used to deploy the TAM metre over some six thousand television sets around India. TRPs are calculated from these samples. Though it is debatable whether this is a good enough sample to give a sense of the real reach and popularity of a television programme, I found my task fascinating.

One thing that struck me as strange was that even in regional channels, the television view ratings remained high until midnight. Kanak TV had significantly lower TRPs than many other channels in Odisha, so there were a lot of things we could work on, and I noted them down in a presentation. Basically, I analysed the lesser rated programmes of our competitors and conceptualized a few new programmes for our channel in the same time slots. I felt that by doing this we could attract more viewers to our channel.

Manas was very supportive of my efforts. He admitted that he didn't know how TRPs were calculated. I told him that I had learned it in college. He had a habit of holding my hand as he led me around. Good thing we were in Odisha; we would have been taken for a homosexual couple at media houses in the metros.

Manas was a very funny man. He made me laugh when he said, 'Like you are doing 28 jobs in 28 weeks in 28 states of India, I eat seven dishes in seven hotels in seven days.' We usually had lunch together in a dhaba near the office. They had a strange system—irrespective of what or how much we ate, it cost us a 30 rupees per person. Whatever weight I had lost on my travels I would probably regain in a week of eating so much rice.

*

My mother had been after me to get married for some time now, and seemed to believe that I would meet someone during my travels. I had managed to avoid the issue. As I still had feelings for Sameen I felt it would be unfair to meet other girls. But now that I had met Sameen after all these years and seen her with her husband, I realized that I should move on with my life.

Meanwhile my mother told me about a girl she had found for me named Pooja. With other information like her schooling and workplace, I was able to find her on Facebook. The very first status message on her wall was: No one can kiss me the way you do. Interesting profile, I thought, and sent her a friend request.

She accepted and sent me a message. 'Do I know you?' That meant the news about our potential match hadn't reached her. I was more than happy to initiate a conversation without any strings attached. Finally, after a string of messages, I asked her if she minded meeting in person. 'Yeah, you can meet me,' she wrote. I loved her attitude; the way she put it was almost as though I had asked to meet a politician. Her next message contained the location: Teapot at Mayfair.

Mayfair, a luxury hotel in Bhubaneswar, had some restaurants and bars. I was waiting at the Lagoon Reception. She appeared the next moment, wearing a knee-length black dress. I drew out my greeting, attempting to cover up my awe at seeing her. She blushed, and then led me to the restaurant.

We walked through well-tended gardens to reach Teapot. There could not have been a better place for a meeting with a girl, and we had a memorable Saturday evening. We sat in the little garden outside, enjoying the water fountain and its rushing sound.

Our conversation began with talking about what she did and how she loved to go partying. She mentioned that the city was in an upgradation phrase, and I laughed. She meant that many of the newly opened restaurants and malls were crowded with over-enthusiastic teenagers, the reason why she had chosen to come to this place where we could sit peacefully and talk.

My most awkward moment was when I had to look at the menu to order. Life is too short to remember all the complicated food names at a five-star restaurant. I usually pass the task on to the person with me and let them order for both of us. She ordered some Italian food and then looked at the drinks section before putting the menu back on the table. I asked her whether she would like a drink. She hesitated at first, and then ordered two glasses of wine. I began the conversation: 'So.' She repeated the same expression with a sigh. 'Soooo.' This made both of us laugh.

While having the first sip of wine, she asked me about my week in Mumbai. Bollywood fascinates everyone and it is the easiest way to start a conversation. Her next question was which Bollywood actresses I had met. Her eyes were glowing while listening to me. She asked whether I had ever gone to Goa during the Sunburn Festival, and I told her about my tattooing job. She confessed that she wanted to get a tattoo on her hip.

Though I had travelled a lot and met different kinds of people, I was a bit surprised by this broad-minded Odia girl. I was enjoying spending time with her, and our conversation gradually took on a more flirtatious tone. Her desire to go to Puri beach kind of turned me on. During my engineering days, couples used to go to Puri to have fun.

It was already eight and it would take at least an hour to reach Puri from Bhubaneswar, and she had mentioned that she had to come back early as she had work the next morning. A series of thoughts marched through my mind. If we went to Puri, there would hardly be any people on the beach that late at night; we were not going for a *darshan* of Lord Jagannath the next day; and we would not be able to see the beautiful sunrise. She smiled at me naughtily and brought my thoughts back to earth.

15. Chhattisgarh

Content Writing for Job Aspirants

Amazing travel stories and the continuous flow of food from hawkers makes a train journey in India very colourful. The calls for morning breakfast and the voice of the chaiwallah shook me out of my sleep early the next morning. I passed a five-rupee coin through a window and bought myself a cup of steaming hot tea. As I sipped the tasteless chai, a middle-aged man in the berth just below mine grabbed my attention. He was scribbling something. Out of curiosity, I peered down to have a look and discovered he was writing in his diary. My curiosity grew. Reading another's journal is bad manners but most of us are tempted when it's right there.

'I woke up early today. I went to the toilet. I am in a train. I brushed my teeth. There was no water in the tap. I had to buy a mineral water bottle and wash my face. I hate this system. So much corruption. Water bottle is very costly. In stations it is cheap. My kids annoy me a lot. They disturbed me all night. I got pissed off and shouted at them.'

I could not read another word as I was trying to control my laughter. Reading another's journal is really fun, especially when one encounters something like this. In school we were taught that it was bad manners to read another person's journal but we humans like being outlaws sometimes.

I was supposed to be noting down all my experiences in a journal. This made me nervous as I would have to write a lot of stories, and here I was disrespecting somebody who had the patience to record his daily routine. It made me feel ashamed. The practice of expressing one's thoughts and emotions in words is a tough job, and I struggle when I try to do it. My next job would be a test of this very skill.

I would be working as a content writer at Netratva Technologies in Raipur. In technical writing, you don't have the luxury of adding excessive words and emotions. All you need to do is express your idea, keeping your words concise and clear. And that is where one struggles. While in school, I always dreamt of being a writer, but I had no idea it would be such a tough job. My English was pathetic. Being from a vernacular medium, I never had the opportunity to gain fluency in the language and so I was never confident about my ability to produce something in English. However, my command over the language increased when I started preparing for the GRE in Chennai. Prior to that, I would always fumble helplessly whenever I tried speaking in English. I would keep away from girls for the same reason during my college days.

*

Ankur was the founder of Netratva Technologies and would be my employer in Raipur. A mutual friend had connected us.

I reached Raipur at eight thirty the next morning. This

was not my first visit to the city. I had been there a number of times before during my intermediate classes. My cousin used to run a mattress shop in Titilagarh and I had accompanied him a couple of times on his business trips.

Raipur is a centre of commerce. Many cities nearby depend on it for business. I would often see people flocking to the crowded electronic market for its cheap rates. Back then, I would always carry a list of gadgets to buy and carry back home, some for my personal use but many to fulfil requests from my friends and close relatives. I was well acquainted with the hand-pulled rickshaws. I put my luggage in one and walked along with it to where I would be staying. Ankur had arranged my accommodation near the office.

Netratva Technologies offered computer courses and prepared final year engineering students and fresh graduates for placement interviews. My job was to prepare a guide book following certain established rules and recommended tips. Since I came from the same background and had work experience in a few firms, it was not a difficult assignment. I was also asked to prepare samples of possible and frequently asked questions. For better comprehension, I prepared a career chart for the students. These classes primarily focused on polishing one's presentation skills and vocabulary. They also helped the aspirants boost their confidence. The firm was doing a good job, empowering people to secure employment.

My work at the office was usually done much before closing time so I had time to listen to office gossip. Indians like to poke their nose into others' affairs, and that's what I was doing. On my last day at work, Ankur and Kshitij, another colleague, took me to a movie. It had been a long time since I had seen one, and as a movie buff, I missed it. We watched *Madras Cafe*. I liked it, especially the manner in which the civil war in the country was handled. Our evening ended at a good restaurant, where we sampled the best food in Raipur.

16. Jharkhand

Discovering Jamshedpur Through Data Entry and on Foot

From Raipur, I travelled to Jamshedpur in the neighbouring state of Jharkhand. The cool morning breeze welcomed me to the city built by the Tatas and named after the group's founder, Jamsetji Nusserwanji Tata, a pioneer and entrepreneur as well as a staunch patriot and a humanist.

My job here would be to work as a data entry operator in the CAT training institute, TIME. This job bought alive memories of my first encounter with a computer. My parents didn't know much about computers, forget Information Technology. They thought of the computer as an advanced typing machine. When I first enrolled in the IT stream during my engineering, my father had no idea what the course was about. He only knew that it had something to do with the computer and so he advised me to join a typewriting institute as he thought it would come in handy. It was only after I joined college that I realized the difference.

Unlike today, very few schools had computers. Although I had not seen one while growing up, I knew something about them from hearsay, and had formed my own perception. I knew this machine was something that made our lives easier, but I didn't know how.

At that time, a new type of fortune-teller flooded the markets of rural India. Crude early versions of humanoid robots installed at busy markets attracted passersby like a magnet. This machine fascinated everybody. There would be an earphone attached to the machine which played a pre-recorded fortune-telling message, the same for everybody, irrespective of sun signs or date of birth. One fine Sunday morning, I got to see it in my village haat. I was probably eight or nine then and assumed, in my excitement, that this was a computer.

After that, for the next couple of months, I would always enquire about it whenever my father returned from the market. With age and education, my perception of the computer changed from a man-like machine to a TV-like box meant to do office work.

One day at school we heard that a few computers had been installed in the District Collector's office. I was curious and couldn't wait to see it. The next day, I left for school early, lying to my parents about some project work. Instead of heading to school, my friends and I went to the Collector's office. As we peeped through the window, we saw a man cleaning a few TV-like machines. And that is how I saw a computer for the first time. I recalled that day when I saw the office boy at TIME dusting the computer monitors.

The institute organized an annual state-level quiz for all school students called the Aqua Rezia Quiz Contest. My job was to enter all the data of the participating students in an

Excel sheet and send it back to the management. My boss handed me a monstrous bundle of data. It was a monotonous job, but one always gets to learn something every time, no matter how dull the task.

Thanks to the data entry job, I learnt a lot about the demography of the city and the names of the different localities of Jamshedpur. Since all the participants were teenagers, most found it cool to add odd epithets to their email IDs. Perhaps this was necessary as the number of internet users had grown dramatically over the past fifteen years or so. Most new internet users would not have been able to register their name alone as an email ID, unless of course they had a unique name, as I did. Also, with the growing popularity of Facebook, it could be seen that based on their email IDs, almost all of them had opted for the social website rather than the more common Gmail, Yahoo, Rediffmail, and so on.

Working in a corporate environment calls for a lot of formality. My boss, Bipin, had served on the HR teams of many companies before he joined TIME. He always smiled, irrespective of the situation, no doubt part of his corporate training.

Bipin was in his mid-thirties. His well-maintained, short curly hair, rimless spectacles, clean-shaven face and polished, formal attire made him look every bit like a corporate manager.

Since I had been entrusted with the job of compiling data for the quiz, I was to accompany Bipin to the schools for the screening tests. Every day, he would tell me we would go the next morning. Every morning, I would wake up early and get ready, but the call never came. Later, at the office, he would apologize, only to repeat the same story. To make matters worse he would try to cover up with a lame excuse. I found it strange and quite unacceptable that he wouldn't inform me in advance in an age when technology made communications so easy. However, waking up at five in the morning gave me time to explore the city on my own.

I prefer walking to taking rickshaws or cabs, especially when I am in a new place. This helps me learn about the place and the people. Jamshedpur is an industrial city, but it has a few good places for a tourist too. I enjoyed my leisure time in Jubilee Park and walking by the Dimna Lake.

There are many other things that most people do not know about Jamshedpur. Other than being an industrial city, it is one of the most well planned cities in the country. It had been selected as one of the cities for 'the Global Compact Cities Pilot Programme' by the United Nations, the only one from India and South Asia.

Jamshedpur is the only million plus city in India without a municipal corporation. Tata Steel runs a major part of the city. Thanks to its culture of promoting culture and learning, Jamshedpur has gifted India some extraordinary talents, including the now-international diva Priyanka Chopra, actress and former Miss India Tanushree Dutta, filmmaker Imtiaz Ali, and singer Shilpa Rao, to name a few. This could be why many of its teenage residents dream of going to Bollywood.

Satyagraha released when I was in Jamshedpur, and what

could be better than watching such an inspirational movie in the place of its genesis.

Jharkhand is one of the thirteen states of India in which the Naxalite rebels have considerable influence. Though their existence has created quite a controversy and their practices have earned them the tag of terrorists, their ideals still resonate with many. Their activities have greatly affected the governance of Jharkhand, and the fact that the state had, at that time, a record of ten chief ministers over a period of fourteen years says it all.

It was a great week overall, but just before my departure I was forced to spend a day in bed due to dehydration.

17. Bihar

Selling Condoms in Rural India

On the night bus to Hajipur I was both excited and a little nervous as I'd heard all kinds of stories about venturing into the interiors of Bihar.

My friend Abhishek from Chapra had given me all the basic information I needed to reach Hajipur. I would be staying there and covering the nearby districts to execute a contraceptive rural campaign as a supervisor, working with the rural division of Percept Company.

When I reached the Hajipur bus stand, I called Ravi, a colleague on the same project. He said he would be there in ten minutes. I was looking for a place to keep my luggage as I was desperate to use the washroom. There was no option but to wait for Ravi. While waiting, a poster next to a paan shop caught my eye. It featured Poonam Pandey in *Nasha*. 'After bringing the World Cup to India, Poonam Pandey will bring *Nasha* to you,' the caption read in Hindi. I was pretty sure this was a campaign directed specifically at the rural areas.

When Ravi arrived, it was on a Rajdoot bike, an old classic model. The moment I saw him, I had a feeling that he was a funny guy. After we shook hands, I asked him about the best lodgings nearby. He asked me to get on which I did, holding my dusty bags as far as I could from his white shirt. There were a lot of lodgings near the Hajipur railway station but Ravi was dismissive about them. They weren't safe, he said, people had died there or their luggage had been stolen.

I had heard about Mayur, a guest house of sorts, a little distance away. The manager sent a guy to show us a room on the first floor. A middle-aged man and a young woman were leaving the room as we were walking towards it. An attendant changed the sheets and made a show of cleaning up. I was so tired I didn't fuss. I just wanted to sleep. I stared at the ceiling fan and thought about my job for the next week. I had always been interested in seeing how marketing worked on the ground and fortunately, I had the opportunity now. I hoped this job would be a different experience; I was excited at the idea of exploring a few villages in Bihar.

The next morning, when I took a good look around the guest house, I felt it would be better to stay in the campaign van for a few days rather than going back there. I headed for the van to meet my colleagues, Veer, Gaurav and Brajesh, who had been working out of it for the past week.

Ravi told me stories about the villages we were passing through, how the law and order situation had improved over the last few years, becoming safer. We passed Dhaman and Chamrara. There were always conflicts in these two villages. Dhaman was a village of Yadavs, and Chamrara, of Rajputs. Fifteen years earlier, four or five Yadavs had been killed in a fight between the two, and the next day, the same number of Rajputs were killed, suspected of being murdered as revenge. Even kids as young as five got a pistol as a toy.

Through most of the journey, we saw flood water had spread across the land on one side, and I was apprehensive seeing the look of the Ganga. Ravi referred to the river with great respect, as Ganga ji.

We finally reached Vidyapati Nagar. Anyone passing by our parked van would see the posters pasted on its sides that carried the message: 'Don't forget to use condoms in those intimate moments.'

Our team's job was to travel to some of the villages, convincing the rural people to sell and use condoms. The van had posters of Deluxe Nirodh, the subsidized condom provided by the Government of India as a family planning measure. The government planned to do some rebranding for this two decade-old brand to make it more visible and accessible in small cities. This initiative was called the Condom Social Marketing Programme. It aimed to make condoms widely available in tea stalls, paan shops, stationery shops, general stores and beauty parlours, in addition to the usual pharmacies.

Veer and I bonded quickly. He told me how the campaigners had covered hundreds of new outlets in the last one week. He showed me few paan shops which already had Deluxe Nirodh promotional sachets hanging on their doors.

We stopped at a village square with a few paan shops. Veer and Ravi headed towards two different shops. The rest of us joined them, each holding a packet of Deluxe Nirodh and one promotional card which displayed ten packets. It was time for the sales pitch.

I followed Ravi. I was interested to see how he would sell

this commodity despite being greeted with a big 'NO' from the shopkeeper. Ravi started out by telling him that he did not have to pay much to stock them, and would make a profit by selling at the market price. The shopkeeper refused. Ravi then explained the rationale behind the campaign, how the government wanted to make condoms available in paan shops and corner stores to help prevent unwanted pregnancies, or diseases like AIDS. The paan shop owner seemed uneasy listening to all this. Ravi's next comic approach was *'Aap use karte ho naa, kahe sharma rahe ho?'* You use it yourself, then why are you so shy?

After a minute's silence, the owner revealed that his son also sat in the same shop, so how could he sell these items in front of him? Ravi asked his son's age, and on hearing it was fifteen, he tried to tell the man that nowadays kids knew all about sex well before that. The man smiled pleasantly but refused to take the condoms. But Ravi had picked up positive vibes and passed him some sachets to hang on the wall.

Veer had managed to convince one shopkeeper, but the other two were unwilling to take the condoms. There were no other shops in that square, so we headed towards the next village.

In the van, Veer explained things. 'See, this condom packet worth two rupees contains five condoms, each worth 40 paise and the retail price is fifty paise. In my village, they sell them at one rupee per piece too, and even then, people will buy them as it is cheaper than any other condom.'

Living in a metro, I had never thought about the importance of cheap condoms and the need for them to be easily available everywhere, particularly in the deep rural areas. By then, most condoms in the upmarket parts of urban centres were advertised as pleasure enhancers with varying flavours and features.

Sex is an integral part of human life, rural or urban. Given India's huge population and low awareness about protection, we need to talk about it instead of feeling shy. There was only one paan shop at the next village. Veer and Brajesh headed towards it while we waited in the van. Ravi said that a sale was unlikely as the owner looked old and orthodox. We wondered how Veer would deal with this.

Veer began a rather random conversation with the intention of eventually winning the man over. But the owner blasted him. He was a respectable man, he said, who would never keep condoms, sanitary napkins or hair remover. Veer didn't take offense. Instead he joked and said that he wasn't there to sell those other items, only condoms. The man got even more annoyed and started shouting.

Veer gave up and came back to the van. All of us were laughing, including the driver. Veer said, 'I know these people very well. They have mistresses, and at home they oppress their wives. They go out to eat chicken but pretend to be vegetarians. Such hypocritical bastards!' I was fascinated by the condom selling, and I wanted to try my hand at it. Ravi told me to observe for the first few days but seeing my enthusiasm, he finally agreed to let me try.

This time the shopkeeper was a younger guy, probably around thirty. The issue was that two brothers owned the shop, and the older one was hesitant about how this would look in front of his younger brother. To my luck, this guy was a jovial chap who took the conversation well. Still, he was not willing to sell condoms along with items like soap, toothpaste, and other daily essentials. I tried convincing him to try ten packets at first. Before he could say anything more, Ravi had hung the sachets on the front door. He was not entirely happy about this, but I pointed out that unless customers knew it was available there, how would it sell?

That was how we spent the week. Whether at paan shops, beauty parlours or in general stores, the stories were similar—father and son manned the same shop; a daughter would sometimes sit in the store so the father couldn't sell condoms till she was married; brothers shared the business; and sometimes there would be no reason given, just a flat NO. Whatever the reason, we tried our best to convince them.

One evening we were at Wahidpur, a village near Samastipur. It had a big market and we tried to sell the condoms at suitable outlets. Due to the flooding of the Ganga, villagers from the surrounding areas had shifted to Wahidpur and were staying in the school. We thought we would halt around there for the night. Stationing our van at the school, we walked to the market to buy rice and eggs. We had carried an oil cooker to make dinner.

While at the market, my eyes fell on a shop where hundreds of mobile phones were charging, all the wires tangled into what looked like an untidy spider's web. Ravi explained that it was a mobile charging point with a rate of five rupees for a full charge. When he added that most of the mobiles belonged to villagers who had been affected by the floods, it was quite an eye-opener for me. This was the year 2013 and mobile phones had become an essential item in rural India!

Back in the van we chatted about our day's activities. Our driver went to speak to those who had been affected by the flood, and Ravi went with him to collect stories. Brajesh and Gaurav told me they were childhood friends from the same village, so they knew each other well. Veer was a good cook. He had made egg curry and rice which tasted wonderful.

Not far from the school, there was a mandap under a banyan tree, probably a village gossip centre. It was ten at night and deserted, so we decided to sleep there on the raised platform. Ravi apologized for the circumstances, saying we could have arranged for us to stay at a friend's house for the night, but most of the families had full houses with their relatives from the nearby flood-affected villages.

*

I asked Ravi how come he had joined this profession. Five years back he had been in a different company when he received an offer to do rural promotions in Jharkhand. One of the places they covered was a village in the Gumla district, a completely Naxal-affected area. One had to cross 12 kilometres of jungle to reach the village. Knowing that Maoists would be watching them, Ravi and his colleagues had removed all the posters and modified their jeep in such a way that no one could recognize it as a government vehicle. It is so strange that in most places in India, you can boast if you are part of a government project, but in others, you huddle in fear.

When they had stopped at a police post, they had been caught by some Naxalites. He asked what there was in their vehicle. Ravi showed him a condom packet but didn't say anything. The comrade ordered his junior to take the whole box and distribute the condoms among the women who were there for a local meeting. He didn't know that they were condoms as he didn't recognize the brand name. He thought they were some food items, so each time he handed a condom to a tribal woman he respectfully did a pranam before handing it over. Ravi and the group didn't explain what it was, fearing it would probably result in rapid death. It was both very funny and very scary.

After some time Ravi and the rest of his group told the comrade that they were hungry. Luckily the Naxalites were busy talking among themselves so they took their chance, ran towards their van and drove off. They were afraid that the Naxals would chase them and if caught they could be killed. Luckily, they escaped.

*

We spent the following days doing the same thing—trying to sell condoms to various shopkeepers, sometimes with some success, often being rebuffed. In between, I put together a document, a sort of guide for myself to understand the psyche of the rural customer.

We had one of our funniest experiences on the last day of my trip. As we passed an animal care centre in Patepur, Vaishali, the driver jokingly challenged Ravi to sell condoms there. Ravi responded immediately, saying that animals do not need condoms. Veer took up the challenge and proceeded towards the animal care centre. We were all curious to see what he would do and followed him. Veer showed the man in charge a packet of Deluxe Nirodh, 'Do you need this for your centre?' Obviously, the response was a no.

Veer's next question was, 'How much does a hand glove cost you?' He was referring to the hand gloves used by veterinarians to check on the pregnancy of cows. The man replied that it cost 10 rupees and each could be used only once. Veer said, 'I will give you a better alternative which will cost you maximum 40 paise.' The man was curious. Then Veer explained how a Deluxe Nirodh condom packet with five pieces cost 2 rupees, so each cost only 40 paise. It could stretch to cover the hand, and do the job of a glove. He even demonstrated! Ten minutes later, the man was ready to buy twenty packets. Veer had created a demand where there was none!

At noon on Saturday we went to Kanauli Dhaba for lunch. Over the week, we had covered almost every village assigned to us. Ravi told the others that I was heading to Varanasi the next day, and everyone got a bit emotional. It was suggested that I go with Veer to his village, near the ancient city of Vaishali. From the moment I had entered the state I had wanted to visit at least one ancient city of Bihar, so this suited my plans well.

We set off for Veer's village. I was very impressed by his ability to recall historical details and explain things beautifully. He shared that he had done History Honours in college.

Vaishali was the capital city of the Licchavis and one

of the first examples of the republic state under Vrijji Mahajanapada. Veer explained each of the terms he used, such as Janapada, which is the stronghold of a Kshatriya tribe, the equivalent of a country or nation of that era. Before the time of Buddha, there had been sixteen great nations known as Mahajanapadas, and a few among them were Kashi—the present Varanasi, Magadha—the present Bihar, Vrijji, Panchala, Gandhara, Kuru. Many of these nations had been mentioned in the Mahabharata too. Lichhavi was one of the famous clans from the Vrijji Janapada. It was considered to be the world's oldest democracy as the king was elected by an electoral body consisting of princes and nobles from the Kshatriya clans.

At the World Peace Pagoda, a Japanese Buddhist temple, we walked barefoot on the marble at two in the afternoon, which was nearly unbearable. Our next visit was to the stupa where we met a Buddhist monk. He told us this was one of the eight original stupas built over the mortal remains of the Buddha. After Buddha had attained Mahaparinirvana, his body was cremated at Kushinagar in a royal ceremony, and his mortal remains were distributed between eight places. This stupa was one of them. He showed us the Ashoka pillars and told us that if we went closer to them, we would find the remains of Vaishali. According to legend, the leader of a group of monkeys had offered the Buddha a bowl of honey at that spot. This is regarded as one of the eight most significant events of the Buddha's life. It was in the same place that the Buddha had converted Amrapali, a courtesan who became a nun.

Veer told me that he was fascinated by the story of Amrapali. People believed that at night they could hear the sound of her footsteps walking around Abhishek Pushkarini. Veer spoke of her as if she were his first love, excitement in his eyes and a blush on his face. He said that Amrapali had been declared the most beautiful girl at the age of eleven, and the king, desiring to possess her, murdered Amrapali's would-be groom and made her the bride of Vaishali.

After that we headed to Veer's village. There was a bed in the courtyard of his house. In front lay their field of crops. Veer went to the tube well and brought me some water, then went inside and came out carrying a baby. That was when I realized he was married. I played with the baby for some time. He was less than a year old. He started pulling my hat, so I put it on his head. It was very big for him, almost covering his face. Before he could start crying, I handed him over to his father.

After dinner, we collected my luggage from Ravi and left for the Hajipur station. I called the others to say goodbye. As Veer and I said bye I gave him a bar of chocolate for his son.

I boarded the train for Varanasi and my new job, that of an assistant at a crematorium. I was looking forward to yet another new experience.

18. Uttar Pradesh

Cremation Sites, Aghoris and Their Reality

If I had been able to, I would have made Varanasi the last destination in the course of my travels. It was strange that though it was my first time in the city, I felt as though I had lived an entire life there before. As I rode in an auto rickshaw, I watched the beautiful sunset, which reminded me of the iconic Ganga Aarti of Varanasi that I had seen in so many films.

Instead of heading towards a hotel, I told the auto driver to drop me at Godowlia Chowk. He seemed furious about this. In the popular tourist destinations in the country, most of the auto rickshaw drivers have a deal with the lodge owners. If they bring customers, they usually get a commission from the manager. Sometimes, if you can make a good bargain, they might even drop you free of cost at a lodge, and get their tips from the manager. The rickshaw guy had been ready to drop me at a lodge at a low rate. When I told him that I wanted to see the Ganga Aarti first, he asked for more money. After paying him, I got down at Godowlia Chowk and walked towards the Dashaswamedh Ghat.

The streets of Varanasi are a microcosm of the city. At

any given point in time you can see people having bhang, a priest with a big tilak heading towards the temple, foreign travellers walking towards the ghat, a dead body being carried to a cremation, people sitting on the pavements and getting their heads shaved, a sadhu baba getting high from smoking a chillum, and all of a sudden, a bull blocking your path. Like Mark Twain wrote, 'Banaras is older than history, older than tradition, older even than legend, and looks twice as old as all of them put together.'

As I walked towards the ghat, the scene became even more fascinating. The Aarti was quite different in real life from anything I'd seen on screen. Because of the recent flooding, the venue had shifted to a high platform above the ghat. Jumping from one boat to another, I settled down to watch. Thousands of pilgrims were shouting *'Ganga maiyaa ki jai'*, salutations to the holy mother Ganga. A few foreign travellers had joined in, mouthing the Hindi words. A Chinese guy sitting next to me asked me to take a picture of him with the Aarti in the background.

I had arranged to meet a Brahmin pandit, one of those who performed the rituals at the cremation ghat. One of my friends had organized it, catering to my weird desire to work at a cremation site. After much wandering around the city, I found the mutth where the pandit was staying.

The mutth looked like some kind of ancient house, and in the middle there were arrangements for a *shraaddha* underway. According to Hindu belief, the priests who perform the rituals after death are not allowed to do any pooja for rituals like marriage or thread ceremony. The Tamashik and Satwik are two different paths of Hindu belief.

I was overcome by fear for a moment. Was this where I wanted to be? Well, here I was. Now the big question was how to convince the pandit about my interest in doing this job. He probably wouldn't understand. So I tried to simplify the whole thing by saying I wanted to write a book on the cremation process, and that was why I wanted to work with the undertakers. The pandit's first question was about my caste. When I told him I was a Brahmin he was furious and told me I was mad for wanting to work with the Dom. The cremators of Varanasi are from the Dom caste, a scheduled caste.

The pandit was not willing to listen to my arguments, so I didn't try to convince him. Because I had come there on a reference, he generously arranged a stay for me, but he couldn't help me connect with the Dom. I was happy the accommodation was near the ghat, but living in the same place where there would be several poojas for dead souls on a daily basis made me slightly nervous. However, I calmed myself and decided to stay there.

The night was a nightmare; I could not sleep properly. Even in my conscious state I had never believed in ghosts but I was afraid as I could feel something peculiar in that place. Even small sounds or the wind blowing disturbed me that night. I recalled how, in my hostel days, we had fun by attempting to call spirits. Since I was sleeping on the floor, the rats in the house disturbed me the whole night.

The next morning a man came to take money from the person next to my room. From their conversation, I made out that he was a wood dealer in the Manikarnika Ghat. I followed him there.

Manikarnika means jewelled earrings. This ghat is named after Lord Shiva, who dropped his earrings there during his transcendental dance. People believe that those who are cremated in Varanasi will be liberated from the endless cycle of birth and death, and so hundreds of dead bodies are taken to Manikarnika Ghat every day.

The ghat was crowded with people carrying their dead on bamboo stretchers. The bodies were wrapped in colourful silk clothes and adorned with flowers. Because of the flood, the cremation point had been shifted to a higher platform instead of along the river bank.

Later, I got to know that at most times this river bank area was reserved for rich people. The natural disaster had made all people equal, for once.

Each stretcher was first immersed in the holy river and then taken towards the pyre. Due to the rains and the floods, the whole area had become slippery and wet. I stepped up towards the cremation platform along with people carrying a stretcher. The alley was so crowded that at one point no one could move and everyone was stuck in the same spot. Even the men carrying the stretcher were stranded. I gestured to one of them to let me hold one corner. I almost dropped my end of it but somehow managed to hold it up.

An elderly man showed us the direction in which to take the body towards the arranged pile of wood. A number of bodies were already burning in that crowded space and the smell made me feel nauseous. After depositing the stretcher I walked away and stood at a short distance, turning back to watch the son light his father's pyre.

I shut my eyes for a moment. I was experiencing so many emotions all together at that particular moment: sadness, happiness, freedom, captivity, bliss, anger, loss and finally love. When I turned my face towards the Ganga and slowly opened my eyes to the cloudy sky, I saw Sameen, her beautiful face surrounded by a black scarf. Eternity crosses the barrier of religion. Whenever I was overcome by any strong emotion, a vision of Sameen entered my thoughts.

I stood there for hours, observing the cremation ground, the piles of wood on the boats, the same that would be turned into ashes in a few hours. I cried as I experienced the ultimate truth and the reality of death.

There were many undertakers at the cremation site. Given their low caste status, people were hesitant to speak to them, and maintained a distance even while handing them the things for the rituals.

One man was grubbing in the ashes, looking for expensive items like gold rings and bracelets. I called out but he didn't respond and continued scavenging. I knew I had to convince this man to let me experience a week at a cremation site. I introduced myself as a student doing research on cremation and asked if I could join him for a week. He looked at me and laughed. 'Why do you want to waste your time? You can't eat properly if you work here.' Then he asked, 'Do you drink? I nodded. 'This is the filthiest job on earth. Bring some alcohol, otherwise you won't be able to stay here for long,' he said. He said his name was Sanjeeb.

Sanjeeb treated his work as any other job, the dead body as any other object. The moment he received orders from his superior, he prepared the bed for the *antyesti*, the last sacrifice. His job was to arrange the logs on which the body would be placed. I observed how he kept the longer logs at the centre and the smaller ones at the ends to make a balanced stack. He kept some logs aside to put over the dead body once it was placed on the stack.

According to the custom at the Manikarnika Ghat cremation ground, the person lighting the pyre has to borrow it from the Dom community, the traditional keepers of the ground. The sacred fire had been kept burning for centuries by the Doms, starting from their ancestor, Kalu Dom, who had worked as an undertaker during the time of Raja Harishchandra.

Raja Harishchandra is said to have had two unique qualities: he kept his word, and he had never uttered a lie in his life. These twin qualities were tested heavily by various circumstances. The great sage Vishwamitra once told the king that he had had a dream in which Harishchandra had made a promise to donate his entire kingdom to him. The king was so virtuous that he immediately donated his entire kingdom to the sage and walked away with his wife and son. The sage then set the king many more tests, which led him to penury and separation from his family. But still, Harishchandra stood by his principles.

Varanasi was the only place outside the influence of the sage, but before the king could go there, the sage proclaimed that Harishchandra had to pay an additional amount of *dakshina*. The king had no money left so he sold his wife and son to a Brahmin. When the money collected still did not fulfil the amount, he sold himself to a guard at the cremation ground in Varanasi. That guard was Kalu Dom, and because a king worked under him, he was given the surname 'Raja'. Thereafter he was called Dom Raja.

Sanjeeb passed me the ghee, camphor and sandalwood powder, which is poured over the cremation pyre. The smell of burning flesh could make any person vomit. One body had been brought from the neighbouring state of Bihar, which meant it had been rotting for some time and thus was more wretched to handle. This often happened because of people's intense desire to be cremated at Varanasi, no matter where they had died.

As I watched Sanjeeb push a half-burned limb into the fire, I asked him whether he were afraid of death. 'Everyone is scared of death, but the truth is that we are all going to die one day. So if you embrace death, death can't scare you. The old have to go for the new to come.'

By evening, I left the ground to rest in the mutth. I had no appetite and couldn't even look at food as the scene from the ghat flashed through my mind, along with the smell of burning flesh.

The next day I decided to take Sanjeeb's advice and have some alcohol before going to the ghat. I went to a bhang shop. There are numerous government authorized bhang outlets in this colourful city. A man was rolling out the stalks of green cannabis, mashing them with some oils and turning them into sticky green balls. I must have been the first customer of the day. A little boy was smiling broadly while he mixed a drink made with those cannabis balls. He said while passing me a glass, '*Bholenath ka Prasad hai*', this is an offering to Lord Shiva. Unlike alcohol, bhang does not work immediately, but it slowly elevates the drinker a new high. I asked for another glass and drank it at one go, '*Jai Bam Bhole*'. The little boy saw that I was getting high and giggled.

As I walked towards the ghat I had to dodge a bull, negotiate some slippery stairs, and generally brave the uncertain streets, all while in my high state. As the old saying about the city goes, *raand, saand, seedhi, sanyasi—inse bache, to sebe Kasi,* which means that hustlers, bulls, stairs and the mendicants—if you can escape from all of them, then you can attain salvation at Varanasi.

Thanks to the water having receded, the corpses were now being taken towards the river bank. When I arrived, Sanjeeb was instructing men to taking marigold flowers off a dead body. He had arranged the wood heap. He looked up and gave me a quizzical look. 'So you had alcohol. I can tell.' I smiled and replied '*Jai Bam Bhole*, I had bhang!' He smiled back, accepting me as one of his tribe. Like him, I wore the same clothes I had worn the previous day, and had no intention of changing for the rest of the week. Sanjeeb passed me a plastic bag of sandalwood powder. We commenced our routine as we had the previous day, peppered with bits of alcohol-fuelled conversation.

I told Sanjeeb about my fascination to meet with an Aghori baba. I said a few of the babas I had seen in the ghat with ash over their faces and body seemed likely to be Aghoris, but Sanjeeb's response was that a real Aghori baba wouldn't walk around in the daylight, nor would he advertise his status. His point was that many of the self-claimed babas were criminals who existed on the fringes of society. I asked Sanjeeb if he had met a real Aghori. He nodded and told me to stay at the ghat with him for a night.

I bought a khamba, a full bottle of whiskey, thinking it would be enough for me and Sanjeeb for that night when I would be staying with him. It was strange to see that even at night the cremation ghat had at least one lit pyre. Sanjeeb was sitting on the ghat near the burning pyre, holding a long stick. I passed him a plastic glass, poured the whiskey and kept the bottle aside. Before I could take my first sip, he had already poured more into his glass. I realized that the bottle would be not enough.

At midnight, Sanjeeb told me to follow him. I was half drunk, so didn't realize that we had walked more than half a mile across the river bank. We stepped into a building through a narrow door. The room was lit by a single fire and I could see a human skull and a few bones scattered about. A half naked baba was sitting next to the fire. Sanjeeb told me that the baba had lived there for two decades. On one side of the room, there were some items like a stained mattress and a dusty blanket.

For some reason, I was not afraid of anything at that moment: the thick tilak of Aghori, the skull kept in the room, the claustrophobic atmosphere and the smoke. The baba's eyes were glowing in the dark. Sanjeeb told me that earlier, he used to visit this baba whenever he faced any evil. After that we didn't speak till the baba finished his meditation, which took about an hour.

I had a thousand questions to ask the baba, including finding out the truth behind all the fantastical tales that were told about them. After a short conversation with the baba, I asked him about the origin of their customs. It was all about finding purity in the filthiest things. 'An Aghori is on the right path only if he manages to remain focused on god even during sex with a corpse or eating a human brain, or doing meditation at a cremation.' This made some sense to me. When children are born they have no idea of right and wrong. They can play with their own filth the same way they play with their toys. As they grow older, they are influenced by those around them and society, and things change.

It is the same with death. At first, kids are unaware of it, only growing to fear it with age. Aghor sadhana is a process of unlearning societal norms, facing death like a very young child, and meditating over *smashan* without any distraction.

I always believed that fear is an important part of human emotion. If fear dies, then one would go out of control, and have no limitations. But this week had made me fearless. Even I lost my fear of death, just as Sanjeeb had. Death signals that the body is just a part of the life cycle. Only the soul is eternal. Like the Bhagavad Gita states, 'The soul can never be cut to pieces by any weapon, nor burned by fire, nor moistened by water, nor withered by the wind.'

Varanasi is a city of contradictions. You can find an Aghori in the filthiest environment of night and pyre wood, and the next morning, a Satwik sadhu doing pooja with sandalwood. On the street, your feet touch the excreta of cows and a horrid stench rises up, and the next moment you smell fresh air perfumed by the sweet fragrance of flowers at the nearest temple. You might not find a salon for a haircut but you will see hundreds of barbers lined up, waiting for clients who want a tonsure. You may hear a lecture on how non-vegetarian food harms your body but you could also see a chicken outlet.

At the ghat, you can see mourning faces around a dead body and ten minutes later the same people are enjoying the sweet taste of rabdi. In front of Kashi Vishwanath Temple, you may see a policeman claiming to be an atheist checking all the devotees entering the temple; the next moment you pass another policeman singing Shiva Purana. When you feel like crying at the cremation ground, you look around to find that you are alone in your sorrow. At the ghat, the wood dealer will lie to the customer about the price of his wares, and the next moment you hear *'Ram naam satya hai!'*

19. West Bengal

From the Potter's Wheel to Bolting from Sonagachi

I took a train from Varanasi to Howrah station. There was a long line of bright yellow taxis parked near the exit. As soon as I stepped outside, a crowd of taxi drivers gathered around, each one trying to get me to take their cabs. The fares they were demanding were exorbitant, and as I began to negotiate, they began fighting over who would take me. As I walked away I met an elderly man who directed me to a prepaid taxi stand.

Kolkata still had a vintage feel to it. The nickname *City of Joy* has stuck ever since Dominique Lapierre's novel came out in 1985. As my taxi honked its way through the busy traffic, the sight of hand-pulled rickshaws, tram lines and old British buildings greeted me.

I had a room booked in a hotel at Park Circus. Rajesh Kankaria, an acquaintance who was a very senior entrepreneur with nearly 30 years' experience, had sponsored my stay in the city. I was perhaps the only mud artist—my job in the city—fortunate enough to live in the posh area of Park Circus while working at Kumartoli. I smiled at the thought.

Kolkata Metro, started in 1985, was the first underground

metro in India. Thanks to its Metro Rail, travelling within Kolkata was not a problem. I checked into my hotel to freshen up and then took a train to the Sobha Bazaar station, from where Kumortuli was within walking distance.

Kumortuli is a traditional potters' enclave in north Kolkata. This is where all the idols of Hindu gods and goddesses are crafted for Durga Puja and other occasions. Durga Puja was just a few days away, and the place was already filled with life-size idols of different gods and goddesses. Hundreds of shops in the area stock the idols.

I arrived at my destination, a studio-cum-shop. 'So you want to work here,' my to-be boss said as I walked in. Before I could say anything, he handed me an *I, Robot* poster and asked me to replicate it. I laughed. At first I thought he was kidding, but I was wrong. He actually wanted me to build a robot. It was like building a rocket without even knowing Newton's laws. I was clueless. The studio had only one Durga idol while the rest were elephants, dolphins, Spartan soldiers, gladiators, and so on. It looked more like a museum than a studio.

I was instructed to join a group preparing the smooth clay required to make an idol. Most of the products were made with fibre or plaster of Paris. An artist named Vishu was my guide for the job. His name reminded me of the story of Konark Temple and its architect, Vishu Maharana.

In the thirteenth century, King Narsimha Dev of the Eastern Ganga dynasty decided to build a massive temple in Konark. According to a legend behind this magnificent temple in Orissa, he wanted it to resemble the Sun God riding his chariot. Twelve hundred craftsmen were employed, but even then the construction could not be completed within the stipulated time of five years. By the twelfth year, the king had threatened to execute all the craftsmen if the temple was not completed within a night. The crown on the Sun God's head was yet to be finished. Everybody was in distress, including Vishu Maharana.

Legend says that the chief architect's twelve-year-old son Dharmapada then saved the artisans by completing the task single-handedly. However, this posed yet another threat to everybody's life as they feared if the king found out he would execute the artisans for not following his orders. They demanded Dharmapada's death but Vishu Maharana protested. He would not let his innocent son face death at any cost. Seeing his father's helplessness, Dharmapada committed suicide by jumping off the top of the temple.

My guide, Vishu, was very funny and made a lot of jokes related to sex. He gave me some insight into how the mud takes on the shape of any object. Whenever a statue of cellulose fibre was to be made, it was first made out of mud. Once dried, a mould was made with plaster of Paris to capture the shape of the object. After the mould was ready, heated cellulose fibre was then poured into it to produce the statue. The worst part was that the mud model was destroyed.

Vishu usually made the mud models, and I was very curious to learn from him. Despite the fact that it would be destroyed later, he still devoted a great deal of attention to making them.

He asked me if I had a girlfriend, and when I was noncommittal, he helpfully informed me, '*Yaha se 200 metre duri mein hi hain, us taraf ... Ek baar jaana zaroor.*' At first I had no idea what he was talking about. Then it struck me that he was talking about Sonagachi, the biggest red-light area of India, which was a stone's throw from the studio.

Hearing that I was in Kolkata, Deepak, one of my college friends, came to see me at Kumortuli one day. He had recently been transferred to IBM in Kolkata. The work I was doing fascinated him. It had been a long time since I had seen a known face and meeting Deepak was like seeing somebody from my family.

I took Deepak for a walk around Kumartoli. Hundreds of photographers roamed around the place, taking pictures. Passing the DSLR crowd was not an easy affair, as they had taken the entire lane for themselves. This irritated us and the obvious question was whether all of them were really photographers or people with lots of money who wanted to be photographers. In the course of our conversation, Vishu had his say on the matter. 'Do all these photographers ever dare to enter that golden lane of Sonagachi?'

'We dare,' we smiled and stated in unison. However, deep inside, I knew how difficult it would be to actually go there. We had had a different perception about Sonagachi during our engineering college days. During our final year, many of my friends had gone to Kolkata especially to explore Sonagachi and had come back with all kinds of stories, some real, others probably fantasies.

Now that we were so close to Sonagachi, we were reminded of those stories. None of the guys who claimed to have visited Sonagachi had said a word about how filthy it was. While some claimed to have enjoyed sex in air conditioned rooms available in buildings called Prembandhan and Neelkamal, others said that they lured the sex workers to perform *mujra* or dance performances, by giving them hundred rupee notes. However, the most stupid and degrading thing that became popular when they returned was that they began rating every girl in the college with prices ranging from 50 to 250 rupees for the most beautiful.

With all these stories in our minds, we decided to explore the area. We started walking along Ravindra Sarani towards Beadon Street. Just before Beadon Street, on the left side of the road lies the golden lane of Sonagachi. Around fifty sex workers stood by the opening of the narrow gully. However, we failed to notice the fine line between the normal world and the red light world, and walked past them, towards Beadon Street. A few metres ahead, we stopped for a cup of tea and started a conversation with the chaiwallah. When we asked for directions to Sonagachi, he smiled and said that we had passed it on the way to his shop.

To our surprise, we found nothing exceptional about Sonagachi. It looked like any other residential area, with dirty lanes and general stores. Deepak and I walked down the lane, trying to avoid making eye contact with any of the girls who stood by the old buildings. Some sat on the steps while a few stared down from the balconies. I couldn't resist for too long though, and finally glanced at a few. All of them had a layer of make-up on, red glossy lipstick painted over their lips to make them look juicier, eyelids painted in different colours and cheeks as red as a ripe tomato. They all flashed seductive smiles when they saw us looking.

Far from the so-called civilized world, this is the place where everyone gets nude, whether physically or mentally. The colours of a brothel are vibrant, but they have a dark history that gets lost in the busy, cruel world. We managed to come out of the lane without facing much harassment. This gave us more courage and after reaching the main road, we decided to go back and walk past it again. A sudden sense of immature joy and excitement grew within us. It was not as if we were desperate to get laid, but we were thrilled to have stepped into a place we had only heard about and imagined for years.

It was dark by now. As we walked back into the lane, a girl tried to lure Deepak, asking for the water bottle he had with him. I cracked a joke, 'Somehow you replenish her thirst,' and both of us laughed. Just as I was about to turn around to leave the place, I heard Deepak calling my name. When I turned back, I saw Deepak surrounded by a gang of six women, two of whom were holding his T-shirt tightly. One stood on Deepak's flip-flops while the others blocked his way. Before I could move towards him to help, I too was surrounded. All the women were sex workers from that lane. From our talk, one of the women understood that we were Odias.

'Are you from Odisha, motherfucker?' We didn't respond. Then the woman said that there were some young girls inside and we were asked to follow them into the brothel. This was getting ugly. Deepak started pleading with them to leave us but they would not listen. I told one strongly built woman who seemed like the gang leader that we were on our way to Kumortuli and had to pass through the area.

She asked me if I knew that the clay for building the Durga idols had been taken from the brothel. I nodded. 'Yes, I have seen it in the movie *Devdas*.'

The women took both of us to a gully with many *kothas* along both the sides. One of the women was holding my hand and leading the way. The building into which we were led into had many small rooms, each with a bed inside. We kept asking them to let us go but they ignored us. Just as they forced us into a room, I stepped on a woman's sari by mistake. This made her furious, and her voice was filled with reproach. We tried our best not to display any signs of fear that would make them more aggressive. One of them asked for our wallets. There was not much cash in them, but they kept whatever they found. Then she asked where we were staying and accordingly left us some money for our return journey.

'Do you masturbate or do you have girlfriends to stop the fire?' We ignored a young girl's comment and fled the place. The moment we were on the main road amidst the busy traffic, we burst into laughter. Even though we had gone there for a lark, treating it as more of a tourist spot than a brothel, we had paid our entry fee to walk through Sonagachi, the golden lane.

*

One of the best and most creative things that I came across during my stay in the city of joy was the Calcutta Photo Tours. This was an eight-kilometre early morning walk which took people around eighteenth-century monuments. An entrepreneur named Manjit Singh Hoonjan has started this innovative venture to show the early settlements of the Portuguese, Dutch, Danish, French, Armenians, Chinese and British, spread across the city.

Kolkata is a melting pot of cultures and communities, a true kaleidoscope of various shades, flavours and sights. The tour took us to the oldest surviving Christian tomb in the city, synagogues which have stood for centuries, Bow Barracks, a Zoroastrian Fire Temple, old Chinatown, old Jewish neighbourhoods, a Jain Temple, a Portuguese Church, and an Armenian Church, all of which depicted the true kaleidoscope of Kolkata.

20. Assam

Learning the Ropes at a Tea Factory

I took the Kamrup Express from Kolkata to Dibrugarh, Assam. For some reason, I had assumed that the north-east would be cold, so while leaving Kolkata, I had put my winter clothes on top in my bag.

Assam was humid and hot, and I felt exactly the way I had while in Amritsar in June. I looked out of the window to observe the people and their clothes, trying to follow their conversation. Assamese sounded very similar to Bengali and Odia. I could follow a bit of Assamese as it was quite similar to Bengali.

My train went past Tinsukia on its way to Dibrugarh. Thanks to the long train ride, I got to meet people from every corner of the north eastern state as then it was the only route that connected all the major points. Many of them were students from Nagaland, Mizoram and Manipur who were studying in other parts of the country. While chatting with them I got to know something about Naga culture. By the time the train arrived at Dibrugarh station at six in the morning, there were hardly any people on board. My only co-travellers were brave soldiers from the Indian army who looked dashing in their uniforms.

After alighting, I had to get to Chaulkhowa. This was where the tea factory I would be working at was located. It was on the way to Dibrugarh airport. The owner of the tea factory connected me with a guy who was staying at the site. It turned out Ajit was from Bihar.

I called Ajit to ask him for directions to the factory. He told me to take a shared auto running along that route from Dibrugarh. Beautiful tea gardens lined both sides of the street, and not surprisingly, Dibrugarh is called the 'tea city of India'. I was guided to the staff quarters of the factory to keep my luggage.

When I went back to the factory, I was introduced to the other workers. The manager ordered black tea for everyone. It was made with freshly dried tea leaves. It was so refreshing that I felt my tiredness melt away. A gentle evening breeze carried the aroma of the freshly cut tea leaves and I was instantly reminded of the numerous commercials that featured magical tea gardens.

In the evening, trucks carrying tea leaves arrived at the factory, and while the others attended to them, the manager gave me a brief introduction to how the tea factory worked. It started with freshly plucked leaves being processed in the factory. Then they were packed into packages of 30 kilos each and distributed throughout India. In a typical small factory with seven to eight workers as most of the jobs were done by machines. The workers just needed to monitor the machines and supervise whenever required.

The tea leaves were poured into a long container, where big fans were used to dry the leaves and reduce the moisture. They were put into small bags and hung on rotating chains which took them into the factory. There, the bags were emptied into the grinder.

When the leaves were freshly ground, they looked green in colour. Then they were passed through a heated metal slider around 30 metres long, and this gradually changed the colour of the tea. After fermentation, the tea takes on a brownish colour. Then the drying dust is separated into different categories of tea. Some of the most popular grades in the market are the larger grains, broken orange pekoe, and the lower grades including fannings and dust.

My job was to empty the bags as they came inside. The grinders produce a deafening noise. Because of heaters inside, the factory was damn hot, and I felt a wave of sympathy for the workers.

I had the opportunity to meet the owner of the factory one day. He was from Gujarat, and he told me the story of how his forefathers had migrated to this place long ago in search of better opportunities. He took me to one of his tea gardens, and explained how the tea picking happened. He hummed the famous song of Bhupen Hazarika, the most popular voice of Assam. The song captures the delicate nuances of tea picking, 'two leaves and a bud':

Ek kali do pattiyan
Nazuk nazuk ungliyan
Tor rahi hain kaun ye
Ek kali do pattiyan

The lifespan of a tea plant is 100 years, so it never betrays the man who planted it. The buds and leaves are called flushes. A plant will grow a new flush every seven to fifteen days during the growing season.

*

One evening, Ajit and I went for a stroll through Dibrugarh as he wanted to buy something. We stopped at a roadside eatery. Ajit asked for a sweet dish and I had papdi chaat. I have never been a chaat kind of guy, but I decided to try some that day. We then went to a movie hall and watched *The Lunchbox*, even though we ourselves hadn't eaten lunch!

At night, I felt uneasy so I decided to skip dinner. My stomach was twisting and turning with severe pain. Ajit came to know about the problem, and promised that he would bring me medicine the next day. But Ajit's choice of medicine was a bottle of cold beer. I'm not sure which medical college he passed out of.

The first thing I did the next day was to call up was a real doctor, my friend Tushar. He first pulled my leg, saying if you change your state every week the 'state' of your stomach will be screwed up. We had been friends ever since the days when we were preparing for the joint entrance exams. He told me it was probably a regular stomach infection and prescribed some medicine. He warned me not to drink any kind of alcohol because it would dehydrate my body.

Even after having the medicine for two days, I wasn't feeling better. I got scared when I saw that my stools were red and had mucus. Looking at my miserable condition, my boss advised me to shift to a guest house in Dibrugarh in order to have quicker access to medical facilities.

After shifting to a lodge named Mourya, my visits to the loo increased so much that I thought I would create a Guinness world record. Funnily enough, I was not feeling weak. I was thankful to the ORS powder for saving my life. Tushar kept calling to check up on me from time to time. When nothing worked out, he gave me the name of another doctor for a follow-up.

The doctor prescribed a different medicine. Five days had passed, but still nothing was working out. I consulted yet another doctor. He gave me a few more capsules to increase the immunity of my digestive system. Tushar kept telling me that curd would be a good alternative to such a capsule. But in Dibrugarh, most of the hotels didn't serve curd.

Finally my search for curd and rice ended at a good restaurant. The restaurant was very classy, and it seemed I was the first person in its history to have ordered rice and curd. It was run by a group of sisters. In the north-east, women are quite visible at workplaces. Many restaurants and shops were being run by women. I was surrounded by many beautiful girls at the restaurant, all of them giving me disgusted looks. A word of advice to the guys: do not order curd and rice on a date.

I learned later that I was suffering traveller's diarrhoea. Traveller's diarrhoea, like love sickness, is not easily curable. I went to a pharmacy where I had the following conversation with the store guy. 'Sir I don't have med-A, can I give you an alternate with same composition?' I agreed. Then he said, 'Sir

I don't have med-B, can I give you an alternative?' I asked him if the only medicine he had was Hajmola.

Frustrated and weak, I bought tender coconut, pomegranate and bananas. On the way back to the factory from the market I started vomiting on the street. At this point of time, I felt for the first time that I had to go back home to recover. I could not see any other solution to my plight. When you are physically weak, it makes you mentally weak as well. When you are mentally weak, it makes you physically weak. You should know the fine connections between body and mind!

It was then that I almost gave up my journey. I thought it would be better to go home before it was too late. In an unknown land, travellers usually enjoy themselves, but this time my situation was very different. I started feeling lonely. It was the first time I considered flying to a destination in my whole journey of 28 weeks. Ajit took me to the airport and we said goodbye.

*

Tushar was serving his first job at the government hospital in Sonepur, my hometown. He visited me the moment I reached. I felt better after having home food. My mother was anxious to look after me, and served me pakhala and curd. Pakhala is a traditional Odia food which is made up of fermented rice soaked in water overnight. I was taking homeopathic medicines too to get over the stomach pain.

After two days, I went to the hospital again for a stool test. Tushar was surrounded by two police inspectors who were accompanying a man who had been accused of rape. It was Tushar's first encounter with the police, so he was a bit nervous working on the documents. When the compounder took the accused to a secluded room to get a sperm sample, the accused gave the excuse that 'sperm is not coming'. To overcome this problem, the resourceful compounder passed him his mobile phone and showed him a porn clip. I thought the police inspector would slap the compounder.

*

I was still recuperating at home. One morning, I heard peculiar sounds. In my village, whenever someone dies, there is a specific kind of dhol that is played just before the body is taken towards the cremation ground. And if you look at the streets, lia or puffed rice is scattered on the road, from which people come to know that someone has passed away.

Out of curiosity, I rushed towards our gate when I heard the dhol playing. The guy who had died was a good friend of mine from childhood. His name was Sujit. I had spoken to him on my last visit home. He was a struggling politician then.

As children we used to perform the Ramleela at his home. I used to be Ram, and he used to be Lakshman. We would play with an abandoned cycle tyre, rolling it through the streets. I recalled those moments when I saw his now lifeless body being carried on a bed. He had become a drug addict. When I left my hometown at the age of fifteen, it was a clean town, but in the last fourteen years a large number of young people had begun to fall prey to drugs and thus destroyed their own lives. It was a growing phenomenon in small towns in India.

After resting at home for some days, I regained my energy so I decided to resume my journey. I had defeated the persistent bacteria that had created an internal cyclone in my stomach. For a self-fitness test, I did a 120-km bike ride and reached my mother's maternal home. As usual, I asked my grandfather how he was. He was as enthusiastic as ever. His answer brought my energy back: 'I am 85-years young and I can walk for 30 km if needed.' Perhaps that was the sign I was looking for. I smiled and told myself it was time to resume my journey.

21. Sikkim

Tossing Mojitos at a Gangtok Bar

I bid goodbye to Sonepur and resumed my journey. I was eagerly looking forward to visiting Sikkim. I would go to New Jalpaiguri and from there, travel towards Gangtok. This city is without doubt one of the most famous tourist destinations in the north-east. One of my friends, Keshav, who is from Gangtok, got me a job as a floor manager at a lounge bar there. I was hoping that working in a bar would lift my spirits!

I fell in love with Gangtok at first glance. Just seeing the cloudy weather, the beautiful roads, the beautiful people made me wish I could stay there forever. I had discovered a home away from home.

I searched for my workplace, Lounge 31A. I thought it was a pretty unique name. I was a little confused by the name but later on I was told by the locals that the lounge was named after the national highway that connects Siliguri to Gangtok. The 31 Lounge had three outlets: 31A Prive, 31A Studio in the Deorali region, and 31A ZP at zero point Gangtok.

31A Prive was rather like a private hang out area, with

a billiards table at the centre. Patrons sat on cushions on the floor, and the tables were low, just half a foot off the ground. The Prive looked like a cosy and comfortable place to have a pint.

31A Studio had a more casual and cool ambience. Raw stones on the walls gave it a cave-like feeling. There was also an in-house band that played rocking music in the evening, and over the week I became really close to them. They earned their money 'in' the bar and spent it 'inside' the bar as well. The songs of the Beatles, Rolling Stones, Bob Dylan and other legends of rock 'n' roll would fill the night air with high energy.

There was also a well-stocked bar to quench the thirst of travellers from all over. The studio was always filled with people from far-off countries exchanging stories and gossip. I could see the poetic types scribbling in their journals, and there were a few regulars who visited the bar to let their daytime worries melt into the night. 31A Studio was a haven for people with a hippie mindset, and offered them music and conversation. What more could one ask for?

As the floor manager at Lounge 31A, I spent most of my time interacting with customers, and taking their feedback. I would rattle off 'the special menu of the day', and learnt to appreciate the art of describing food that can make customers' mouths water. I loved talking to young people on various topics. The bar was a happy meeting ground for all kinds of people, and I was fortunate to become a part of so many stories and to hear them share their many dreams. It is only in the informal setting of a bar that people open up to you completely.

The students of Sikkim Manipal University had made the lounge their favourite hang out. One day, 31A Studio was packed with the young college-goers. A hip-hop artist was expected to perform that evening. The DJ spun the latest rave tunes and a group of guys began to dance. The strobe lights flew all over the room, and everything became a blur. The best part of talking to an intoxicated young soul is that they nod their heads even when it is not required, thus symbolizing their coolness.

Most of the youngsters wore black, as if it were some kind of theme dress they had chosen. They were all taking photographs of each other. A few posed with their middle finger up, and others with the index and little finger flexed, again a symbol of their coolness. Every few minutes, one of them would call for a group hug. I was expecting the hug to end up with their collapsing on the ground.

There was one guy named Saroj who seemed to me the smartest one. I started talking to him. He recognized me when he saw my golf cap. That day, three English newspapers in Gangtok had featured my One Week Job story. He was excited to speak to me. Like many young people I'd met, he began by saying, 'You know what, I love travelling. Look, you have done so many jobs, why don't you take my interview?' It was more of a demand than a request. He was in his fourth year of electrical engineering. I didn't know much about the subject, but I asked one question. 'I would like to build a self-sustained village for 200 families. How much electricity would I need to develop? Which power would be cheapest for me: wind or solar, and how much will it cost?' He had not been expecting such a question and blabbered something. I was not expecting him to give the correct answers, but it was fun.

He introduced me to one of his friends from Delhi, who was already quite drunk. I asked her whether she liked this bar better than anything she had visited at home. 'You can't be yourself in Delhi because people are always judging you. I feel free here,' she said. She waved her hands in the air. 'Free like a bird.'

Ongmu and David became my best friends during that week. Ongmu was the counter manager. She loved watching Korean soaps on YouTube. She was an independent married woman, and gave me some good insights into the women-centric culture of the north-eastern states. Ongmu usually worked till late at night and went home in a shared taxi. Many small bars in Gangtok were run by women, and disturbances were extremely rare, no matter how drunk the patrons were. That definitely says something about their control.

David was the bartender at 31A Studio. He was planning to move to Dubai soon, where he had been offered a similar job. Meanwhile he was training his replacement. David made the cocktails so fast that it looked like some kind of magic trick. He would throw the bottles up into the air, catch them deftly and pour the alcohol into the glass, moving the shakers to the rhythm of the music.

I enjoyed observing David's tricks. I wanted to learn how to prepare my favourite cocktail, the mojito. He taught me, step by step. I crushed mint leaves and lime to mix them properly. Then I added more lime wedges and sugar, and mixed it again. David poured the mixture into a shaker filled with ice cubes, and drizzled rum over it and showed me how to move the shaker so that it would make the cocktail tastier. When it was finally poured into the glass, the drink looked carbonated. A good shaker can make powerful bubbles and change the taste of the cocktail. Every morning, one hour before the bar opened, things would be hectic with the staff cleaning up and getting everything ready for the day ahead. The first song played in 31A was usually *Om Mani Padme Hum*, a Buddhist chant. The meaning of the chant is 'You can transform your impure body, speech, and mind into the pure exalted body, speech, and mind of a Buddha.' I got completely addicted to the song during my time there. I would stare at the Buddha statue for hours, a depiction of a contemplative, resting Buddha, who almost looked like he was dozing off. I thought this was the perfect image for the bar.

Yankesh, the owner of 31A, had every quality of a dynamic entrepreneur. He adapted to things quickly and executed them if he thought they would benefit his business. We usually sat together late at night, after all the customers had left, and discussed possible ways to attract more business. One such idea was a food and culture fest to promote ethnic Nepali, Lepcha and Bhutia food and culture.

I could easily connect with Yankesh's journey as an entrepreneur. He had also been an engineer. His face glowed when he spoke about his first step towards 31A, how when still a final year engineering student, he had borrowed money and started his first lounge outlet at Zero Point, one of the famous areas in Gangtok. His business had grown over the last seven years, and now he hoped to set up ventures outside the city. He was a good businessman with strong political contacts, though he himself was very modest and soft-spoken.

On Diwali night, there were only a few Indians among the crowd at 31A Studio. There were many foreign backpackers though, chilling here in the course of their world trips. I asked Yankesh which kind of crowd he liked better, foreign or Indian. 'Backpackers don't have much money,' he said honestly, 'but they have made my 31A famous. I love them for that. Young Indians come regularly and they spend more money here. I love the colours of the crowd more than the money.'

While talking to Yankesh, I noticed a beautiful woman who was passing by our table. She looked vaguely familiar. It was Celine, the French woman I had met during my week in Rajasthan! She looked surprised at seeing me there and asked, 'What are you doing here?' I had not expected her to remember me, and smiled. 'You change jobs very quickly, don't you?' I knew she was pulling my leg and I just nodded and smiled. We had a short conversation about the last few trips she had taken, and then I joined Yankesh again.

Another businessman had joined Yankesh while I was gone, and he offered me a drink. I politely refused. Yankesh interrupted, saying, 'Don't worry, you are not working today. Today is Diwali night!' When I accepted the drink he added, 'In Sikkim, it isn't polite to say no when someone offers you a drink. At least have a small one.'

A group of girls in traditional attire entered 31A studio and took the stage. They started a Nepali folk song called

Bhailo. This is a Diwali song that is sung during the festival of lights, or Tiharas as it is called in Nepali. Yankesh informed me that these groups would go to different houses, restaurants and other business outlets on Diwali night to sing, collect money, and give blessings for prosperity. I enjoyed the music so much that I took a video.

The next performance was by a group of teenage musicians who sang some beautiful, romantic songs and made the Diwali evening a memorable one.

Yankesh and I talked for a long time over glasses of red wine and whisky. In the background, the singers crooned one of my favourite songs.

I could search the whole world over
Until my life is through
But I know I'll never find another you

When they wrapped up for the night, the singers were paid their fee which they spent in the bar itself. I chatted with the guys about their musical journey, and what they wanted to do, what had brought them together to form a band, how passionate they were about music. Most of them had long hair. I asked the lead singer his name. Like a true SRK fan, he said, 'Rahul. *Naam toh sunaa hi hoga.*'

22. Arunachal Pradesh

Storytelling with Little Monks at Tawang Monastery

Post Diwali, I was on my way to Arunachal Pradesh. I took a taxi to Siliguri. From there, I had to take a bus towards Tezpur in Assam. The bus started in the afternoon, and was supposed to reach the next morning. But at midnight, it stopped in the middle of nowhere, near Bongaigaon. When I woke early in the morning, I could see lots of buses and trucks stuck there.

The NDFB, the National Democratic Front of Bodoland, an armed separatist group, had called for a 36-hour bandh as a protest for their cause of a separate state for the Bodo people. It had affected public transport, trucks and private vehicles, all of them forced to a standstill on the road.

There was an early winter chill in the air. Many of the people in the buses got down to stretch. There was an abandoned house nearby, but when I got a chance to go to the washroom, I almost vomited. It was extremely dirty. I managed somehow and wished the vehicles would start moving soon.

One of my co-passengers from Tezpur introduced me to the bandh culture of Assam, which had become a hurdle for the region's economic development. He was explaining how the idea of separate statehood had taken root in this area. The Bodo people had been inhabitants of the area for a long time, and were very much against migrants. Our bus was stranded in the middle of the Bodoland Territorial Autonomous Districts, comprising Kokrajhar, Baksa, Chirang and Udalguri, and we still had a long way to go. A few others were arguing that the bandh was only a rumour. After another six hours, a police van escorted the vehicles and helped us cross the disputed area.

Once I reached Tezpur, I looked for a cheap guest house to stay the night. In the morning, I would begin proceedings to get the Inner Line Permit (ILP), a special pass that everyone, even Indians, require to enter Arunachal Pradesh. The owner of the guest house told me that it would take a day to get the pass from the Deputy Commissioner's office. I looked for travel agents who claimed that I would get it at the Bhalukpong checkpoint, the border of Assam and Arunachal Pradesh. He was backed up by a taxi driver, who told me I shouldn't waste a day in Tezpur.

I booked a seat on a shared taxi and got a corner seat. I was still a little unsure about getting the ILP pass for Arunachal Pradesh the next day, but I told myself, *jo hoga dekha jayega*. After eating some delicious fish fry and grabbing a pint of beer, I set my alarm for five the next morning and got some sleep.

Tezpur to Tawang is a drive of around 400 kilometres, but it takes at least thirteen hours to go through the hilly routes. Everyone in the ten-seater Sumo had the ILP pass except for me. When the Sumo stopped at the Bhalukpong checkpoint, everyone showed their pass. Since I didn't have a pass, the driver told me to go to the nearest booth and talk to the guy to get the permit made. After taking a photocopy of my identity proof and some photos of me, it took an hour to get things done from the nearest office. Thankfully, the other passengers cooperated and hung around the market to have breakfast.

Finally, the Sumo started off for Tawang. After crossing Bhalukpong, there seemed to be few civilians but there were many military camps all along on the route. The man sitting next to me was an SSB jawan, and he told me that the Sashastra Seema Bal, the border guarding force, was very active in that area.

By the time we reached Tawang it was dark. The driver asked where I would be getting down, but I was clueless; the person I needed to contact couldn't be reached. I told the driver to drop me somewhere in the centre of town.

By the time I got off the bus I felt that it was already ten at night but it was seven in the evening. I found a guest house and told the owner I needed to meet someone named LG. She figured that stood for Lama Gurung, and told me I would have to meet him in the monastery. I was to spend a week as a storytelling instructor at the famous Tawang Monastery.

The guest house owner asked if I needed anything. It was very cold and I skipped dinner, and went to bed instead. The person I was supposed to meet was still not reachable, and I had no idea what would happen the next day.

After a freezing bath the next morning, I started to stroll around town to find my way to Tawang Monastery. I stopped at a teashop to warm up. The tea here tasted very different; it had butter, salt and special tea leaves.

I asked an army man for directions to the monastery. As I climbed up the hilly trail he had pointed to, a huge palace-like structure came into view. The Tawang Monastery complex is the second largest of its kind, ranking after Lhasa in Tibet. There were numerous prayer flags waving along the route. The flags of different colours were arranged from left to right in a specific order: blue, white, red, green and yellow. Later, I learnt that they represented the five elements: sky, air, fire, water and earth.

I passed through the gate, and on my right, I saw an old Tibetan man spinning the prayer wheels with reverence. I had visited a number of monasteries in Ladakh that also had large metal prayer wheels set side by side in a row, which people could spin by sliding their hands over each one.

Right behind the library of the monastery, I saw hundreds of little monks in maroon robes praying and chanting mantras. Behind them, the beautiful Himalayas towered, watchful. This was going to be my workplace. I loved it already.

Before going to the school, I walked up a few more steps towards the temple where I could see many tourists taking pictures. The main assembly hall of the temple had a 27-foot tall Golden Buddha. Both sides of the wall had thangkas, paintings made with cotton and silk appliqué depicting the Buddhist deity. The wooden architecture of the roof and pillars inside the temple had many intricate designs. This was one of the most beautiful monasteries I had ever visited. It belonged to the Gelug school of Buddhism.

There was a museum next to the temple which housed many objects of this 400 year-old monastery. I studied the photo of the 14th Dalai Lama who had fled from Tibet into India in 1959. There were a few more pictures from the 1962 Sino-Indian War. During that time, this monastery had been controlled by Chinese troops for six months, till Tawang once again came under Indian control. China still claims that Arunachal Pradesh is a part of South Tibet, and belongs to them.

I went to the office of the monastery to talk to the Trust Administrator. He was very supportive of my desire to conduct storytelling workshops, and referred me to the principal to take it forward.

Back in the school area, a group of little monks were sitting on the ground in a circle. The teacher sat on a chair in the centre. Unlike the monks, the teachers were not in red robes. They were not monks.

I chatted with a teacher who had been working at the school for the last fifteen years. He gave me a little insight into the little monks' life. In Tibetan culture, parents traditionally send their second sons to become monks. Shelter and food are provided by the monastery. The monastery itself is run on contributions from the local people, funding and donations. I spoke to him about my One Week Job project, and he offered to introduce me to the principal.

The principal of the school was a lama. He wore the traditional red robes of the monks. He spoke very little and simply nodded to indicate his approval of my idea. After that, a teacher took me to a large hall in the school where I could conduct the workshops. On the way we passed classes of LKG and UKG-age monks, shouting loudly because their teacher had stepped out for a moment.

I wondered how these little monks felt later in life when they understood they had been signed away to celibacy before they could even comprehend sexual attraction. The teacher responded in a very mature way. 'We always teach them what they should do and what they should not do. But there is always a difference between what one should not and what one cannot.'

Here in the school, the monks studied till the eighth class and then moved to Sarnath for higher studies. The hall where I would be conducting workshops was a large one with a red carpet on the ground, similar in colour to the monks' robes. Half the wall's height was panelled with wood, while one side of the hall had a white wall. I thought this would be a good place to experiment with Fetcha Kucha.

A friend and I started Fetcha Kucha, a storytelling concept, inspired by the very popular Japanese storytelling technique of Pecha Kucha. We would stick thousands of pictures on the wall and tell the participants to come up with a single story connecting a few random pictures. It is an impromptu storytelling session, where the audience plays along with the pictures. Whenever I have done this Fetcha Kucha storytelling workshop, it has given me new insights into the human mind and its creative powers.

I started hunting for my collection of pictures. I went to

an internet café and got black and white prints of the pictures at a decent price. Once I had bought scissors, sellotape, cardboard and paper for the session, I was ready.

I spoke to a few of the monks to understand their psychology. The Tawang Monastery has hostels for the 450 monks who study there. I went to one of the monk's rooms and saw that it was made of wood, while one corner had a bed with a printed bedsheet over it. The monk's name was Sangay, and he had joined this monastery when he was just six years old. When I asked him why he wanted to become a lama, he said that lamas are the spiritual masters, and not every monk is a lama.

I chose to conduct the workshop for children in the classes of six to eight together. When I distributed the colourful pictures to the young monks and told them to paste them on the wall, they did so very enthusiastically.

Sangay was there as well. I explained the rules and regulations of the workshop and he made everyone understand them properly. I divided the storytelling session into two parts: in one, they would choose any ten pictures and build a story from them, and in the other, I would point out ten pictures and tell them to build a story.

In most of their stories, the children were clear about developing a protagonist with a name, which I liked very much. Romantic relationships, marriage, having kids, all of these were part of their stories. There was one story that I thought came close to my ideals of living one's passion. The story went like this.

There was a small kid called Rahul who didn't like to

study. He was the naughtiest kid among his friends. He always wanted to play. When he got the time, he loved to paint. His mother loved him very much. His father was an engineer, and he wanted Rahul to be an engineer too, but Rahul had always wanted to be a painter.

Rahul started going to college. (The monk pointed to the picture of a beautiful girl with a garland.) This is Rahul's girlfriend, who loved him very much. She even told him to paint a portrait of her. Finally, Rahul became a successful painter. He and his girlfriend got married. They had a kid and lived happily ever after.

I loved the stories told by the little monks. Whenever they talked about girlfriends they giggled and looked shy, just like any other boys their age would. Despite the fact that they lived the secluded lives of monks, they were quite aware of the world outside.

*

I enjoyed the week in Tawang. Walking down to the war memorial was a great outing and I did that on a couple of afternoons. I loved the place and had good conversations with the soldiers who took care of the memorial. In Tawang the sun could set at half past four or even earlier, and my body clock was soon attuned to the local sunrise and sunset timings. Most of the shops closed by half past six in the evening, and so I had my dinner by seven before returning to the lodge.

On my last day there, a group of young travellers from Mumbai arrived at my guest house. When I struck up a conversation, they mentioned they were going to Bum La the next day. They insisted that I join them, as I could not miss visiting Bum La. The pass, about 32 kilometres from Tawang, was via a rough road. It got colder as we went higher. The view was beautiful from Bum La. We spent the day taking in the breathtakingly clear lakes, the majestic mountains, as well as the war memorials and bunkers.

While coming back to Tawang, our car got stuck in the mud. Other vehicles tried to pull it out but nothing worked. Finally, an army truck pulled up and helped us out.

The same group of travellers were off to Kaziranga the next day and they were kind enough to offer me a seat in their car, so I managed a ride halfway to my next destination.

23. Nagaland

No Job Vacancies for Strangers in a Gun House

Pine trees were all around with the odd rhododendron bush. Yaks were grazing leisurely. While passing the Sela pass, these views and the snow covered forests and mountains could take anyone's breath away. We enjoyed all this while I rode back to Tezpur with the Mumbaikars. They continued on to Kaziranga while I took a local bus to Dimapur in Nagaland.

My bus took me along the Kaziranga route. I could see the dense forest lining the road. On the way to Dimapur, the temperature rose so high that it began to feel like summer again. The fluctuating temperatures and my poor eating habits on the journey had made me feel unwell. I was once again subject to stomach upsets. But this time the medicine worked well and I recovered fully in a day.

My friend Piyush from Kolkata had connected me with a family in Dimapur. When I told Mr Jain, the hardware store owner, about my desire to work in a gun house, he laughed at the idea. He knew it would be almost impossible to convince a gun house owner to hire me but he wished me luck.

When I started walking down Church Road towards Eros Lane, I could see the gun houses, ammunition, and the gun repair shops that lay along one stretch. It seemed as though people here were more dependent on these shops than grocery stores for their daily needs. Dimapur is often in the press because of its illegal arms and ammunition business.

The first shop I dared to approach had no customers at that point of time. I told the man at the counter that I was a writer, and I wanted to gain one week's experience in his shop to know more about a gun house. He said no. When I tried to persuade him, he pointed his weapon at me and asked if I really wanted to write about a gun house. As I left, I could still hear his laughter ringing in my ears.

The next experience was also very bad, but at least this time the owner told me why he was saying no. Recently, the Nagaland police along with the Assam Rifles had arrested some men for smuggling weapons to insurgent groups, and that was why people were more cautious these days. Having failed at my declared intent, I came back to the hardware store to try my hand there for a week.

The owner told me more about the gun culture in Dimapur, of how the locally made rifles could be bought for as low as 5,000 rupees. Many shops sold products like air guns, which did not need a license. Nagaland is also known as the land of guns as almost every family possesses at least one muzzle-loading gun or licensed guns of different types. Tribal people acquire the guns for hunting. It was normal for households to have as many guns as the number of males in the house.

Luckily I got a job at the hardware store as an assistant. I had to locate the items the owner wanted to fulfil his orders. All the workers in that shop were from Uttar Pradesh. The oldest one was in his mid-fifties. Jiten made our work very easy, as having been associated with the shop since its opening he knew where everything was kept. The store had a huge repository of items like tools, plumbing and electrical supplies, cleaning products, houseware, utensils, paints and garden products.

In Dimapur, women often did the hardware shopping themselves, unlike in other parts of India. I also noticed that many people bought blue paint. Jiten informed me that most commercial buildings in the city were painted blue. He didn't tell me why.

The timings of the shop were from seven in the morning to five thirty. I didn't find the job very interesting but a job is a job. We didn't need to use our brains much. All jobs aren't fulfilling, sometimes we just work for survival. But the most important thing is to be happy and adapt oneself and one's humour to derive some pleasure from the menial tasks too. I heard the same thing from Jiten.

The owner of the shop had migrated from Rajasthan some forty-five years back. I learnt that nearly all the businessmen in Dimapur are from outside the state. Marwadis and Jains are no strangers to business opportunities in the region. Before the Second World War, the commercial trading and business hub was Kohima, the current capital of Nagaland. But during the War, the major businessmen shifted from Kohima to Dimapur, and thus made it the new commercial capital.

I had heard a lot about the Hornbill Festival, the most popular festival in Nagaland. It was held annually in the first week of December, and preparations had already begun while I was there. My boss showed me a collection of photos of the last festival. The Naga people were dressed in traditional, tribal costumes. Other interesting pictures showed pole climbing, a chilli-eating competition, spear fighting and courtship dances. The whole album was colourful and tempted me to go back some day to see it for myself.

*

It was not difficult to communicate with people in Nagaland as many spoke English, the official language of the state. While the British were there in the early nineteenth century, it was American missionaries who, in the early 1870s, set up schools and opened churches. The region was thus exposed to the English language, a western education and Christianity comparatively early.

In the evenings, I used to spend time in a guitar showroom a few shops down the street. Samuel, the man who ran the shop, looked quite like a rockstar himself. He had been born and brought up in Dimapur.

Samuel spoke about how western culture had evolved in Nagaland over the last few decades. Till the 1980s, the only entertainment was the radio, but when the television came, it took a backseat. Maradona became an obsession with youngsters during the 1986 FIFA World Cup. Around that time, video parlours opened up and people had access to Hollywood and Chinese martial arts movies.

In the early 1990s, when cable television reached Dimapur, it opened the doors to the contemporary western world through programmes like *Santa Barbara*, *Riviera* and *Baywatch*. These became instant hits. Slowly, many more youngsters were drawn to western culture. Their taste in music changed as well.

Samuel stopped in the middle of the conversation and asked me, 'Do you know we have a Guinness world record for the largest electric guitar ensemble in Dimapur?' I had no idea of what he was talking about. He explained that in January 2013, some five hundred participants had gathered in the Agri-Expo Ground of Dimapur to set a record. A few of the famous songs they played were the Guns N' Roses version of Bob Dylan's iconic *Knockin' on Heaven's Door*. He took out his guitar and played a few chords.

> *Mama put my guns in the ground*
> *I can't shoot them anymore*
> *That cold black cloud is comin' down*
> *Feels like I'm knockin' on heaven's door*
> *Knock-knock-knockin' on heaven's door*

Samuel became a good friend after two days of long evening conversations. 'I hope you have tasted the bhut jolokia chilli,' he teased me. I had heard a lot about the Naga chilli so it was one of the first things I had tried when I got there. I had no intention of eating it again!

'Let me take you somewhere new,' said Samuel one day. We went to the dog market of Dimapur. Dog meat is a favourite among almost every tribe in Nagaland; many eat it in the false belief that it increases sexual potency, while others eat it for its iron content. At first, I had been horrified, but then I rationalized it to myself, thinking that the same could be said of many other kinds of red meat that people eat around the world.

One day we were roaming around Hongkong market, the Mecca of fashion. It was a congested market with loads of hawkers trying to pull you towards the shops. This market is famous for cheap clothing imported from South East Asia. I must say that people in Nagaland are very fashion-conscious. The youth of this region are well in tune with international trends. Western fashions came here in the nineteenth century when many of the tribes of Nagaland were baptised and converted to Christianity.

Samuel had strong opinions and could be quite frank. He pointed out the cultural imperialism that was the result of the television and the print media. 'We young ones, we have all dissociated ourselves from our past. We all proudly say we are Naga but we don't know the language; all the educated people speak English. Over time we have forgotten our history and culture, and we are losing our identity. We watch and imbibe Korean pop culture instead of building our own.'

While hopping from one shop to another, we saw a young girl who smiled at us. She wore a translucent black and white animal print shirt, and a calf-length black skirt. When the girl went to the next shop, Samuel joined her and passed some comment that made her laugh. This process was repeated till he told me to stay in a particular shop and wait for him to come back. I didn't understand how he had won her heart in half an hour.

When they reappeared, Samuel's left hand was locked with her right hand. He introduced her as Gloria, and said she was from some hill district. The three of us, travelling on one bike, stopped in front of a budget guest house and went inside a room. Samuel went out to bring some alcohol, leaving both of us behind.

Gloria and I slowly started talking. I asked whether she had a boyfriend and she said, 'Everyone is my boyfriend.' I liked her open and honest attitude. We sat in silence for some time, and then she told me a Naga story.

'The first man became lonely and went to God to ask for a companion. God told him to mould something from earth, but it did not go as he expected. So he called it a tiger, while his next attempt turned out to be an elephant, then a bird and so on. After many attempts, he finally gave up and sat up by a pond, and seeing the reflection in the water, he reached and touched it and thus created woman. The two fell madly in love and thus is remains today.'

This was one of the best stories I heard throughout my trip. She was very attractive and if Samuel hadn't appeared at the right time, I don't know what would have happened. Gloria was quiet for some time. We had a few pegs each and talked about Dimapur. They were getting a bit cosy so I thought it would be best to give them some privacy. As I made an excuse and was leaving the room, Gloria gave me a warm hug.

24. Manipur

The Indian Army, AFSPA and the Citizens

Dimapur is the only place in Nagaland that does not require an Inner Line Permit, but to go towards Kohima enroute to Imphal, an ILP pass is mandatory. I got one from the Deputy Commissioner in Dimapur, and started off the next morning in another shared Sumo.

We didn't stop at Kohima, but the driver told us that we would halt at the Manipur border. The farm lands on the hills, the lush green forest and the road seemed very serene. There were pineapple plantations along the step hills. Almost as though it was an intended contrast, the area had a heavy military presence which took away all thoughts of liberty. Insurgency groups like the NSCN-IM, the National Socialist Council of Nagaland-Isak Muivah, were very active in these regions.

A passenger sitting next to me told me about the illegal tax racket run by some insurgency groups in Nagaland. Excluding the police and army employees, every government employee had to pay 20 to 25 per cent of his monthly salary as an annual tax to these groups. Even the transport and commercial trucks entering Nagaland were asked to pay up. Our driver paid some money at a checkpost that looked almost like an official police post. Later I learnt that it was operated by some militant groups. 'There are many more insurgency groups in Manipur,' the passenger said. It was a frightening thought. I hoped I wouldn't encounter any problems during my stay.

It was not for the first time I had heard such things about Manipur. Many of my friends had warned me against going there. There were many ethnic militant groups with different demands, who often fought among themselves. Some of them wanted to gain independence from India and form a new country.

We stopped for lunch at the Mao Gate, the border between Nagaland and Manipur. I had rice and eromba, a Manipuri fish dish, and then I roamed around the vegetable market to look at the variety on sale. A few of them were new to me; even the local tomato looked very different from the ones you see in most parts of the country.

*

I had a job in hand for my week in Imphal. I would be working as a journalist at Manipurtimes.com. I had a word with my boss, James Khangenbam, before reaching there. He gave me a warm welcome and invited me to stay in his home.

The vice president of a local political party had been shot dead and a bandh had been declared the day I arrived. There had been a bomb set off in the market a few days ago too, which had led to major unrest. Such events were not uncommon in this city.

James took me to his house where I left my luggage. His home felt like my own. It was similar to houses in other small towns, with an open courtyard in front and a little garden next to it. There was a tulsi plant near the door, and a diya as well. The majority of Manipuri people are Hindus who follow Vaishnavism. While the classical Manipuri dance style is known across the country, the Krishna Raslila is a popular theatrical dance form in Manipuri culture.

We headed back to the office. James had done his journalism degree in Delhi and had a good year of experience in the media before joining this online media portal which was a very popular in Manipur. I was quite impressed by its Facebook page and noticed that it had almost one lakh followers. It was a funded start-up being run by a few media enthusiasts from Imphal. The office had a chilled-out environment, like many other start-ups I had seen.

James introduced me to his friend and colleague, Ngangbam, who had just come back from covering a story. After we exchanged pleasantries, he headed to his desk to write his story.

James gave me basic information on journalism; how to write a report and file a story. He taught me the five Ws and one H: What, Where, When, Why, Who and How. To underline his point, he quoted a poem by Rudyard Kipling.

I keep six honest serving-men
They taught me all I knew;
Their names are What and Why and When
And How and Where and Who.

*

When we came back from the office, there was no power in the house. We sat on the floor to enjoy a candlelight dinner. James introduced me to his parents. His father spoke very little but smiled a lot as we chatted. James's mother asked about my family and my travel experiences while she put rice on my plate. We had rice, dal, fish fry, sougri (a stew made with greens, dried fish and other ingredients) and chilli chutney.

James persuaded his mother to speak in Bengali as her education had been in the Bengali medium. He told me how the original Manipuri script was destroyed at the beginning of the eighteenth century by a king and the Bengali alphabet had been used since then. Even the local newspaper printed its articles in Bengali. In Odisha too the medium of education had been Bengali before it was changed to the Odia language.

When I woke up from my slumber the next morning, James was sitting next to an iron pot containing burning charcoal, which he called a meiphu. I could see the breath coming out of my mouth when I greeted him, it was that cold. I brought a bamboo chair and set it next to the meiphu. James's mother placed a large tea kettle over it. First I thought it was for tea, but it was water to brush our teeth!

James's mother made tea which felt like heaven on such a wintry morning. The sky was beautifully blue, the clouds drifting across it. I felt I was far away from the polluted metros. The very next moment, I saw an aircraft leaving a white line across the blue sky, contradicting me thoroughly.

*

I had heard of Imphal's Imas Market, run by ladies, many times before I had come here. James was writing a story about it, so we went there on the way to the office. The Imas (mothers) Market was exclusively for women vendors and housed around three thousand of them. A few male hawkers had tried to set up their stalls but the women's groups had appealed and they were forced out. James interviewed a few people in Manipuri, while I recorded the proceedings and took photos.

The market was split into two sections on either side of a road. There were all kinds of household and grocery items, vegetable, fish and fruit in one section and handlooms in the other. All the women in the market wore the traditional wrap-around skirt called phanek, and a shawl.

As we came out I saw a sculpture of a kneeling elephant with a warrior putting one foot on the elephant's head. The sculpture, known as SamuMakhong, depicted the very popular story of a real Meitei king.

James asked whether I had heard the song *Qutub Minar* by the Dewarist band. It is a rebellious song that clearly seeks to expose the central government's discrimination and negligence towards Manipur. The lyrics were about a thirst for revenge, of how a person brought the Qutub Minar in a train to Imphal and installed it next to the SamuMakhong. The people of Manipur believe that if you wrap a phanek around a papaya tree, it gives fruit; similarly, the singer Akhu wanted to drape the Qutub Minar with a phanek, hoping to get better conditions in the state.

Since 1980, Manipur had been placed under the Armed

Forces Special Powers Act (AFSPA), which granted special power to the Indian military. This act had led to numerous atrocities. The local people had protested against the gun power of military rule countless times, and Irom Sharmila had taken up the struggle, and had been on a hunger fast for years. She had been fasting since 2000, right after the Malom Massacre in which ten civilians were shot and killed while waiting at a bus stop. The incident was allegedly committed by the Assam Rifles. There were many allegations against the Assam Rifles, including accusations of raping women at gunpoint. In 2004, Manipur erupted in protest and some women stood naked in front of the Indian paramilitary headquarters in Imphal, protesting the rape and murder by the military.

In my week there, I realized that in the last ten years, the media had made considerable efforts to share stories of what had been happening in the state, and hopefully, it would lead to an end to AFSPA at the earliest.

*

I enjoyed the perks of being in a media office, of gathering knowledge about many incidents in Manipur and learning the different angles. A media person knows a lot of things that never come out in the mainstream.

James asked a new employee whether he had managed an interview with a Manipuri actress. He was due to submit it that day. The guy complained that the actress was refusing to schedule the interview and had cancelled twice already. When James told him to call again, he was hesitant to do so. In response, James gave him an awesome lesson. 'See, they are celebrities and they can have attitude, but we can't. People love to read about them, so we write about them. Do people love to read about us? Cut your ego down and call her again.' Before the new guy could do so, James called the actress and fixed the interview right away.

I went along for the interview with Soma Laishram, a popular model, actress and a singer. Soma, who had acted in more than thirty Manipuri films, had started her career as a programme presenter with Doordarshan.

We met Soma at her home. She was wearing casual jeans and a T-shirt and looked so beautiful that I couldn't help staring at her. She might have noticed that I was mesmerized by her beauty, and she smiled when I greeted her. On television commercials, a beautiful Indian girl is always presented as a fair and lovely North Indian. But I must say that she was my definition of beauty. No wonder she had won the runner-up title in the Mega Miss North East Beauty Pageant in 2010.

*

James's mother called us when we were on our way home. There was news of a scarcity of salt in the state, so she wanted us to get a packet. James found out through his media network that it was a rumour, and laughed at the people queuing in long lines in front of shops to procure salt.

Back at the house I got a call with some bad news. My parents had met with an accident and my mother had been badly injured on her face and hand. My immediate reaction was to drop everything and rush back home. My parents hadn't called me because they didn't want me to disturb or worry me. But my sister couldn't keep it a secret and told me everything.

When I called my mother, instead of telling me about the accident, she asked, 'How you are and where are you?' I almost cried. I shared the news with James's mother. She comforted me and told me that my mother would be fine, that I was about to complete the journey. I just had a few more weeks left, I should be strong, and this bad phase too would pass. I felt like I had found a mother in a home away from home.

On James's mother's advice, the first thing we did the next day was to visit the Govindji Temple and Kangla Fort, the palace of the ancient Manipur kingdom. Situated at the heart of Imphal, it is a moated palace with a water body surrounding it. The sculptures of two dragons represent the ancient emblem of the Meiteis.

While coming out of the Kangla palace, I saw a big hoarding for an upcoming polo tournament. I never knew that polo originated in Manipur, and was known locally as Sagol Kangjei.

James took me to the World War Two cemeteries, which contain thousands of graves of British and Indian soldiers. Japanese armies had attempted to destroy the Allied forces at Imphal and invade India, but they were driven back into Burma with heavy losses. The graves have been marked with small stone markers and bronze plaques chronicling the sacrifice of dauntless warriors. Many had the soldiers' names and a message from their families. Some of the bodies had not been found and above one of these graves was the epitaph: 'A soldier of the 1939-1945 War, Known unto God'.

From there we went to a concert venue where preparations for a musical event were underway. Manipurtimes.com was the media partner for the music festival which was to take place the next day. I would have liked to stay back and attend it but I had already booked a ticket to my next destination.

James introduced me to many of his friends. One of them was a photographer named Tiken. He wanted me to taste the local alcohol called waiyu. It looked like water but gave a stronger kick than Goa's cashew fenny. James complained about the taste of the waiyu, and said that it had changed over the past few years. I had very little since I was to travel the next day.

Tiken had to stay back at the concert venue so he suggested we take his bike to go home. I didn't know that Tiken's bike wouldn't respond to any gear after the first one. James knew about it and laughed while I drove through Imphal at night at that slow speed.

I loved the way I got love from Imphal, the new friends I made there, and the people who had become my own in no time.

Tamam rishton ko main ghar par chod aya tha
Fir uske baad mujhe koi ajnabee na mila

~ Bashir Badr

25. Tripura

Launching a Portal with Student Entrepreneurs

The direct route from Imphal to Silchar was not safe because of the insurgency activities in that region. James advised me not to go through that route. Instead, I took a flight which landed in Agartala, the state capital, in about 50 minutes. I could see the border between India and Bangladesh from my window seat.

Tripura is one of the largest rubber-producing states in the country, and on the way, I could see rubber plantations with bowls hanging from the rubber trees to collect the latex. As I travelled across the hilly terrain, I fell more and more in love with the scenery. There was nothing but greenery all around and the word pollution seemed non-existent. The people of the north-eastern states certainly enjoy nature at its very best.

After a journey of some forty-five minutes by road, I reached a place called Kamalghat. I was on my way to the university located there. A quarter mile ahead stood a tall white building. My rickshaw stopped before a massive white wall on which I could see 'The ICFAI University' painted in bold black letters. This would be my twenty-fifth job.

I saw a well-built man waving at me from the gate. As he came forward to welcome me, I realized it was Pranjeet, my employer for the week. Pranjeet and I had met on Facebook and then connected over phone calls. It took me some time to recognize him in person as his hair was much longer than it was in his Facebook profile picture.

A final year engineering student bitten by the entrepreneurship bug, Pranjeet and three of his friends had started an organization to supply ethnic and customized fashion products from the north-eastern region to the rest of the country. They wanted to launch an e-commerce portal for their organization. My job was to help them as a technical advisor and to get their online portal live.

As Pranjeet guided me to the University hostel guest house, the three friends joined us. Lakshmi, Rajdeep and Abhijit were the co-founders of the start-up. All of them were engineering students. Their enthusiasm reminded me of the drive that had propelled me and several of my friends in college, when we felt like we could succeed at anything we dreamt of.

If college is a school of fun then hostel is the temple. I could feel it the moment I stepped in. I could hear voices singing in unison, and somebody was playing the guitar. As I passed the community hall on the way to my guest room, I could see hundreds of guys sitting inside and cheering for Team India. A live cricket match was on between India and Australia. Again, this brought back memories of sitting with my friends, hurling abuse and encouragement at the TV screen as we shared the joys and sorrows of sports matches together.

The beauty of working in a start-up and living in a hostel is that you have no fixed timings. We worked whenever we managed to sit together till late at night. The first day at my work station was more of fun than work. The founders had named the site after traditional Assamese jewellery called Zangfai, no wonder since all of them came from Assam. Zangfai is usually made in the shape of a locket, and worn by Assamese woman.

First, we had to register the website's domain. Unfortunately zangfai.com had already been taken. However, the boys were keen on sticking with it. Also, they didn't want to sacrifice the dotcom tag and replace it with something else. Finally, after a lot of discussion, we decided to register it as Zungfai.com, which sounded very similar to how the local people pronounced the term.

Thanks to my prior experience of working with an e-commerce site, I was able to help them buy the space and configure the site for the purpose. For this, I was familiar with the OS commerce software, but they wanted to go with a new technology platform called Magento. It took me a few days to understand the Magento configuration and then we made the basic website go live.

Together, we came up with a game plan for the week ahead, and set about dividing tasks. We discussed various aspects of design, colour combinations, planned a rough outline for the logo and so on. One of the hostel's residents was really good at Photoshop, and was willing to help.

Working in a hostel environment is not about enjoying breaks; instead you enjoy working between breaks. The students had a platform called UDDA, the Union for Discussion of Developmental Activities. UDDA topics ranged from Modi to Shahrukh Khan to Deepika Padukone, everything popped up but the talk never failed to come back to the college girls. There were campus rumours of hook-ups and break-ups, as there are in any college. Though I didn't know all the people they were gossiping about, I enjoyed the talk as much as any of the others.

Another fun thing at their campus was the mystery blogger. No one knew who was behind it, but every day a new story would pop up, talking about an incident that had taken place. All the students had funny codenames, such as Chasmees, Padhaku, Mirchi, Mr Bond, and so on. The most popular girl on campus was referred to as Laila, and when Pranjit spoke about her, he blushed. Lakshmi and Rajdeep were fellow sufferers, and Rajdeep revealed their plan to do a dance at the college function: *Laila teri le legi, Tu likhke le le.*

After a week of hostel food, my employers planned to take me out for local cuisine. We strolled around the city. Agartala is a small city and doesn't have much traffic so it is almost unpolluted compared to the bigger cities and metros. The Ujjayanta Palace stands tall and firm in the centre of the city. The white marble palace is an architectural marvel that once was the official residence of the royal family. It had been turned into a museum.

The reigning party had made its presence felt, loud and clear, in the main square of the city. The red flags of CPI-M signified the Communist party's domination in the state of

Tripura. It had ended four decades of insurgency and ensured peace and communal harmony.

I had heard from my father that during his college days, many of his fellow students wore red shirts supporting communism throughout India. Today, those same people's kids were flaunting top-class brands such as Armani and Gucci. Capitalism had completely won over communism in independent India.

The guys took me to a tribal village where I got to taste a few KokBorok dishes. We indulged in some locally brewed rice beer, and then stopped for paan on the way back to the campus. The paan had a squeeze of lemon, a new taste for me. It was sour, but it was interesting and I enjoyed it. I complimented the paanwallah.

We also dropped in on a few local artisans and weavers. Pranjeet and Rajdeep asked them if they would be able to make specific products for their site. They became quite professional during the discussion, and I couldn't help but admire them. Money is always a constraint, but true entrepreneurs never let it affect their hopes. I could see the same spirit in these students.

On my last night, I was invited to a thanksgiving party. Of course, it wasn't for me. The students of the campus had organized it for their fellows. There were couples dancing, singles hitting on the beautiful girls and then there was another group who thought of nothing but getting drunk, dancing and losing themselves in the music. In the blink of an eye, one week had passed.

26. Mizoram

Bike Mechanic by Day, Insurgency History at Night

I travelled from Agartala to Silchar. I had planned to get another Inner Line Permit (ILP) here before moving on to Mizoram. I was in Silchar when I heard that elections were on in Mizoram. There are a lot of disturbances in the hills during election time, resulting in frequent bandhs. I had no option but to stay back for a day.

The bandh turned out to be a blessing in disguise. Silchar is a small city in the Barak Valley of Assam. I spent my extra day roaming around Silchar, eating local food, watching a movie, and doing some window-shopping. I was surprised to see a number of stores selling wedding outfits, including one that stocked only sherwanis. It looked as though a lot of people got married in the city every year.

The next day I applied for an ILP for Aizawl, Mizoram's capital, and booked a shared taxi to get there. After a less than satisfying lunch at a small roadside eatery, we drove to the border checkpoint. The police checked to see if anyone was taking alcohol into this 'dry state', where alcohol is prohibited. They found that one man—the person next to me—was actually carrying a bottle in his jacket. I felt sorry for his loss.

Mizoram

I reached Aizawl in the evening. The sun was nowhere to be seen on the horizon and a fading light welcomed us on our entry into the city. James had connected me with Rcho, the founder of Aizawl Thunders, the oldest Bullet Club of India. He owned a Royal Enfield showroom-cum-workshop, which was to be my next work station. My job for the week was that of a mechanic. It is every bike-loving traveller's dream to own a Bullet and travel around the world to its sweet song. My One Week Job India project had brought me to a biker's temple and I could not ask for more.

Problems have been my constant companion since birth, and it is only when no problem blocks my path that I feel something is off. Aizawl was no exception to this rule. My employer's number was not reachable. I kept on trying but had no luck. I spent the next hour searching for a cheap lodge. None of the doors I knocked on had a room available. To make matters worse, the cheap lodges and guest houses were at a much higher altitude than the streets. The climb was exhausting for a person from the plains and since I had to carry my luggage as well, it took an extra toll on me. I had no energy left. I was panting like a dog and I felt my heartbeat and heavy breathing could be heard a mile away.

I enquired about every possible job opportunity from whoever I passed but all I got was a 'No' each time. Finally, I surrendered. I knew I had to do something but I was completely blank about my next course of action. It was getting dark quickly, and I decided to take a break.

I found a place to sit on the footpath, where some street dogs gave me company. I was watching the cabs going by and noticed something strange. Here, everybody seemed to drive politely. Nobody honked unnecessarily, as they do in other parts of India. Nobody rushed or overtook other vehicles. A biker tried to overtake a lorry, and honked once, asking to pass. The lorry slowed down and let the bike pass. Once the biker passed, he gave two quick horn blasts, as though he was saying 'Thank you'. The truck responded in the same manner as though to say, 'You're welcome'.

A gentleman passing by noticed me and stopped to ask about my business in the hills. After hearing about my project, he offered to help me find accommodation. Just then my phone rang. It was Rcho. I heaved a sigh of relief. I told him where I was and Rcho gave me directions to his place. I could not pronounce the name properly so he sent me a text message: Sikulpuikawn. This was the school area. In ten minutes I had reached the Royal Enfield bullet showroom called Lawma Enfield.

Rcho is a fine man who also happens to be an avid traveller. Thanks to his love for and fascination with bikes, he has made friends from all over India. We found that we had a large number of mutual traveller friends. He invited me to stay at his residence, which was just above the showroom.

Rcho lived in a joint family with his parents, wife, two sons and a daughter. We had a nice conversation over a simple, homemade meal of rice, dal, boiled vegetables and fish.

After dinner, Rcho asked me whether I was tired and wanted to rest. I was feeling more cold than tired, and wanted to get inside a blanket. It was so cold in Aizwal that I didn't want to remove my socks.

The view from the French window was stunning, one of the most beautiful scenes of my whole journey. A million bulbs illuminated the city of Aizwal. I could almost see the entire city and a million bulbs lighting up every household and shop, each seeming to bring the twinkling stars from the sky to the land. It seemed to me nothing less than paradise. I slipped into the soft and warm bed, looking forward to a wonderful experience over the next seven days.

Rcho was a walking encyclopaedia on the Royal Enfield and a big fan of the Bullet. He himself owned seven Enfield bikes. He shared a brief history of the Bullet, from its beginnings in the Redditch factory in the United Kingdom to the first assembling factory in Chennai. After the UK-based company shut down permanently in 1967, Enfield India took the license and became the sole manufacturer of the Bullet with the rights to export them throughout the world. Royal Enfield is now the oldest motorcycle brand in the world, and still sticks to its original design. It has only gotten better with time.

A Bullet owner loves his bike more than anything else, probably more than the lady in his life. I felt privileged and happy to flirt with those machines for a week. Most of the popular bikes in India are manufactured with Japanese technology and don't make for an emotional connection with bikers, asking for almost no maintenance. But in the case of the Enfield, there is often a strong emotional bond. I could see how much Rcho loved his bikes, and I looked forward to learning from him.

The workplace had three sections: an exclusive showroom with the bikes and biker's accessories, a spare parts shop next to it, and the workshop where the machines were repaired. As a maintenance mechanic with no prior experience, I was assigned all kinds of tasks to assist the lead mechanic.

There were seven of us in the workshop. I was the oldest but the least experienced one, with most of the mechanics being in their early twenties. My co-helpers were speaking among themselves in the Mizo language, all except for one who was from West Bengal. I had been assigned to help him.

My job mostly entailed cleaning the spare parts, greasing the chains, checking out the brakes, engine oil changes, and such things. I enjoyed the work and being in the midst of the bikes. The best moment was when, after the maintenance, a bike would leave the compound, producing the typical Bullet sounds.

On an average, there were ten bikes per day coming in for repairs. Sometimes we had a lot of work when a bike was brought in after having met with an accident. In one such case, the bike looked so terrible that I thought it would not be possible to repair it. But the manager of the workshop scrutinized it thoroughly and finally accepted the job.

The manager's name was Krin. He was also an avid traveller who had attended many riders' meet-ups. He told me a lot of stories about his adventures, and even his way of speaking was very similar to Rcho's.

There were a few beautiful Mizo girls working in the showroom. All of them had straight beautiful hair, and every lady was a head-turner. I knew no Mizo of course, so conversations were limited.

*

From what I gathered people there had an early lunch, rather than breakfast. I usually had lunch at ten before going to the workshop. In the evening, over dinner, I would chat with Rcho. He was a very interesting person, full of stories and travel adventures.

His love for football had led him to name his elder son Fernando after the famous Brazilian footballer. His second son was named Sinzi Tiki. When Rcho's son Fernando was very young, he had an imaginary friend named Tiki. But one day, his imaginary friend died after falling from a chair, leaving Fernando broken-hearted. He would listen to no one and keep crying for days. Just around that time, Rcho's second son was born. To bring Fernando back to reality, Rcho named his younger son Sinzi Tiki. Sinzi means second son in Japanese. His younger son was born in the year 2011, when Japan had been struck by an earthquake. The name Sinzi was a form of respect or homage to the millions of people who had suffered on the island nation.

Rcho's family was lovely, and they took me into their hearts. In the evenings, the family would come together to watch a popular Korean soap, which had been dubbed in the Mizo language.

Like father, like son. Rcho's father was as interesting as Rcho himself. He was a history professor and co-author of a book called *Mizo Uprising*, along with his daughter Rini. We would often spend time discussing the history of Mizoram. From 1895 till India's independence, Mizoram was part of the British Empire. Until 1986, it was a part of the state of Assam before it attained statehood.

I am always curious to know about the evolution of insurgency in different states. I didn't want to miss the opportunity of learning about the historical background of insurgency in the Mizo hills from none other than a history professor, JV Hluna.

He told me that it had all begun with an ecological phenomenon called Mautam, which means the bamboo death. The hills of Mizoram are covered with bamboo forests and every 48 years, it blooms with flowers. Its high-protein seeds lead to an explosion in the black rat population in the forests. The massive numbers of rats destroyed the food supplies of the villages as they moved through the fields eating the crops. This led to acute food shortages and a famine.

In 1959, history was repeated with the 48-year cycle and the bamboo started flowering. The Assam government's handling of the famine and provision of relief was extremely poor and hundreds died of starvation. The Indian central government too didn't help. A group of citizens formed the Mizo National Famine Front to provide relief to the starving rural population. Later it renamed itself MNF and began taking up political issues like integrating the people from Mizo-inhabited areas.

Making Assamese the official language in the Mizo Hills, the government's consistent refusal to grant more autonomy and grant separate statehood to the region were a few of the major reasons that led to the outbreak of insurgency. The Mizo uprising that continued for twenty years became a violent rebellion against the federal government, which ended with separate statehood in 1986.

'We didn't know whom to complain to at that time,' said Rcho's father. 'We were part of Assam, but they didn't listen to us. The communication medium was not that great, and we didn't know whether news of the dire situation and the steps that had been taken by the Mizo National Famine Front was reaching other parts of India.'

I really enjoyed talking to him. Another interesting story was about a community called Bnei Menashe, which claim to be descended from one of the ten lost tribes of Israel. After getting evidence of the customs they followed, a few started practising Judaism. Claiming to be Jews, they contacted the Israeli government and after years of interactions on their claim, it was accepted. Many migrated to Israel and a few joined their army. Around two thousand Bnei Menashe migrated to Israel in 2013. Here, I saw the opposite of what I had seen in Himachal. There, thousands of Israelis came to India to unwind after their mandatory army service by doing yoga and trekking, and here, people travelled in the other direction!

*

Six wonderful days passed just like six hours, and soon it was Sunday. On my final day in Aizawl, I got an opportunity to visit the Mizoram Presbyterian Kohhran, the largest church in Mizoram, in the company of Jecelyn. Jecelyn worked as a receptionist at the Lama Aizawl. She was beautiful, had a sweet voice and deep blue eyes. She told me that I had to visit the church at least once. I could not say no to the beautiful lady.

I was feeling feverish that Sunday morning, maybe because of the climate change. When I woke up my feet felt colder than ice. I rubbed them to try and warm up, freshen up and reach the church on time.

While Jecelyn took me around to show me the scenic beauty, I could feel many eyes following us. She must have noticed but probably assumed it was because she was with a vais, an outsider. I cracked a lame joke, 'You can call me vais, but not bhai. It hurts me whenever a beautiful girl calls me brother.' My week in Mizoram ended on a beautiful note.

27. Meghalaya

Working Among HIV+ People in Shillong

My mini odyssey had made me feel more complete as a person, not only because of all that I had seen and experienced but also because I had learnt to adapt to most situations.

The continuous travel and climatic changes had started to take a toll on my health. Since the afternoon, I had been feeling feverish. It would have been sensible to take a break and rest for some time, but disrupting my travel plans at this late stage would have made me mentally more ill and tired. I could not afford to let that happen to me at that point of time. I wanted to complete my odyssey as soon as possible. Once I was in the next state, Meghalaya, I could say that I had visited every state of India. Though one state, Madhya Pradesh, was still on my list, I had been to a couple of places in the state before.

Rcho's mother had given me paracetamol tablets when I refused to stay back. She advised me to take it if I felt my temperature rising. I was touched by her concern. It was a Sunday so there wasn't much traffic. The fever came back while I was waiting for my Sumo so I popped a paracetamol and hoped to feel better.

Travelling in the hills is peaceful as you don't hear many vehicles honking unnecessarily, unlike in the cities. I was fully drenched in sweat for some time, probably because of the effect of the medicine. The guy sitting next to me kept the window open in spite of my pleas and those of others to shut it. The cold December wind was striking my face, and finally I lost my composure and blasted the guy.

A couple of hours out of Aizawl we met with a road accident. Two guys on a bike were driving their bike at a very high speed and hit our Sumo at a hairpin bend. The sun had set by then, forcing us to rely on the vehicle's headlights as the only source of light.

All of us got out of the cab and ran towards the bike. Seeing the accident, I forgot about my fever and joined the others in the rescue operation. The driver had no injury, but the one who had been sitting behind him was unable to stand. He had suffered an injury at his waist. We suggested that they get a lift from another cab and rush him to a hospital. A crowd had gathered by then and was getting bigger. Luckily we were able to get them a lift in a car driving back to Aizawl.

We resumed our journey. By the time we reached Shillong early the next morning, my fever was gone. I felt proud as I had now visited every state in India, with just one more to go to complete my '28 jobs, 28 states' project!

It was too cold for me to bear, so I rushed towards a tea shop. Before I could take a sip of the tea, I felt feverish again and had to vomit. I was in no condition to walk. When I looked back at my heavy luggage, I wondered what I was doing. But then I reminded myself of my mission, and regained my energy.

Meghalaya

I took a break of two days to recover from my illness, and spent my time reading about Meghalaya. It was fascinating to learn that this is the only state where property inheritance is matrilineal among some communities, although at one time it did exist among some communities in Kerala as well.

In Meghalaya, married men stay with their in-laws instead of bringing their wives to their family home. The women control almost everything, be it the household or business. In other words, 'a man is the defender of the woman, but the woman is the keeper of his trust.'

Shillong had been the former capital of Assam when Meghalaya was still part of it. Later the Garo, Khasi, and Jaintia hills were combined to form the new state of Meghalaya.

*

My contact in Shillong was Bimolota, who worked with the UNDP, the United Nations Development Programme. She had connected me with an organization called MSNP+, an NGO working with HIV positive patients.

One of the things that I found unusual and special about MSNP+ was that all its workers, be it the founder members or the ground level workers, were HIV positive. I was a little nervous about working with them at first, as I felt my immunity was low post the fever.

They taught me about INP+, the Indian network for HIV+ people who suffer from AIDS. Similar organizations include NSNP in Nagaland, ASNP in Assam and MSNP in Meghalaya. These are social movements conducted by and for people living with HIV (PLHIV). They also worked at enforcing recognition for the human rights of HIV+ people in India. They had waged a long and intensive struggle against fear, ignorance, prejudice and despair, and stood firm to show courage, insight, acceptance and hope for hundreds and thousands of people living with HIV.

When life shuts one door, another one opens. Well, that is what happened to my employer and the founder of MSNP, Agui. Agui was in the noble profession of teaching, but in the year 2006, an incident turned her life upside down. Everything changed when her husband who was once a drug addict tested positive for HIV. Agui initially feared ostracization from society, but finally they decided to get another check-up done in their home state, Manipur.

Their worst fear was confirmed when the test results once again came out positive. It was a bolt from the blue for the family. Agui decided to take the test, which too was positive. Their children's future was at stake and no prayers seemed to work.

However, the wave of life doesn't end with a trough. They were sure about one thing: no matter how difficult it would be, they had to think about their children. They decided they would help those who, like them, had been struck by this difficulty. It was not an easy task for an HIV+ couple to stand against society. There were numerous hindrances in their way, and at times they felt that they were about to lose the battle. But every time they thought of their children, they regained the courage to fight on.

After a lot of struggle, pain and failure, they succeeded

to bring people suffering from AIDS together under one umbrella to give them psychosocial support. That is how the society called MSNP was born. Agui would say, 'While people say AIDS divides people, it is this very virus that connected us.' It is only because of people like her, with her spirit, that such social taboos can ever end.

I worked at MSNP as a volunteer. My job was to assist the group in various awareness programmes, getting statistics from the hospitals, keeping records in the office, and taking part in the counselling.

MSNP is primarily associated with organizations like the Integrated Counselling and Testing Centre, or ICTC. This is a place where a person is counselled and tested for HIV, of his own free will or on the advice of a medical practitioner. This programme had been started in India in 1997 and there were more than 4000 testing centres operating all over the country from government hospitals. Even today, very few people know about their HIV status. The challenge is to make all HIV infected people in the country aware of their status so that they can adopt a healthy lifestyle, access life-saving care and treatment and avoid further transmission of the virus.

Agui's husband had been infected with HIV because of his habit of using unsterilized injection needles to take drugs. This is one of the most common ways in which it is spread. I met a couple of other guys who were HIV+ who said that they had been least concerned with hygiene when on drugs. They usually passed the syringe from one person to the other. The virus was then transmitted through sexual intercourse. If the man was infected, chances were his partner would be infected too.

Till today, there is no cure for HIV+, but there are drugs to suppress and stop the progression of the disease. The standard antiretroviral therapy (ART) is the most widely used one. There is an ART centre of NACCO in every major city in India. HIV+ people who have an immune measure CD4 count below 350 should take the ART therapy.

I learnt a lot from a doctor I met in Shillong. She was a fresh graduate who was also actively associated with MSNP. After she gave the ART to an HIV+ patient, I could not stop myself from asking her what would happen if that needle touched her body. At first, she laughed and then told me of an experience she had already faced during her earlier training period. Due to lack of caution while injecting a patient, the needle had pierced her body. The incident frightened her to the core, but she didn't panic. There is a prophylactic period of fifteen days in which to prevent the virus, after going for an ELISA test. I was unaware of such measures. I would have turned the world upside down if such a thing had happened to me. That's what separates a doctor from a common man.

*

It was two weeks before Christmas and the whole of Shillong was in a festive mood. I could see festive decorations in the churches, streets, shops and houses. The smell of delicious cakes was everywhere.

MSNP organized a pre-Christmas lunch for the people associated with it. Though HIV+ people are viewed as avoidable by much of society, here they were treated as normal human beings. We worked together, ate together, joked together, and shared the stories of our lives. It was just like living with an extended family. In that very short time I too became a part of their lives or rather they became part of mine. However, it was not easy to see the agony in their eyes, the pain that remains unexpressed within their hearts. I could feel it but all I could give them was a bit of company. I wished I could be of more help.

We would talk about many things over lunches and dinners. Agui inspired everyone to fight the virus, take their ART on time and defy discrimination. She made sure her soldiers didn't lose hope and give up, and that they fought the disease at every step of the way. As I watched her, my respect only grew with every passing moment. She really knew how to make people see that life was worth fighting for.

28. Madhya Pradesh

From a Real Estate Firm to Dhuandhar Falls

One chapter closes and another begins. My next and last destination as part of this One Week Job India journey was Jabalpur in Madhya Pradesh. I checked the routes and found there was a direct train from Guwahati. There were no tickets available and I didn't want to waste time hanging around so I took a bus to Patna instead and then a train to Jabalpur from there.

On the way back from Shillong I could see pine trees standing tall by the roadside and clouds kissing green slopes. Rows of crosses, whitewashed over the many graves in disciplined rows along the slopes of hill, came into view. Wild flowers and creepers had covered a few of them.

As the cab passed through hill towns, there were many stalls selling fresh areca nuts, beetle leaves, pineapples slices, jars of pickled bamboo shoot and wild chillies. A newly-wed couple sat beside me, probably returning fresh from their honeymoon. They whispered in each other's ears all through the drive.

I kept admiring the amazing landscape. The bends in the road, however, were torturous and deadly. We passed an overturned truck and a trailer which had been driven off the road. As soon as we entered the plains, the roads were barely visible because of the dust.

It was the start of winter but Guwahati was still hot. Industrial smoke had replaced the refreshing cool breeze of the hills. The noise and traffic made everything more annoying. After about two-and-a-half hours we reached Guwahati.

My cab dropped me in Paltan Bazaar. I found myself in the middle of a market lying along the busy Guwahati-Shillong road. It had a lot of hotels and bars. Hawkers lined both sides of the road selling almost everything. Restaurants were partially full. All of them had their menus hung outside. Kebabs and chicken were cooking in tandoors. They were also displayed on skewers hung up so that they could be seen through large glass windows. But inside the restaurants, dust and flies over the dining tables were a common sight. Young men were posted outside to lure passers-by.

By the time I reached, it was around two in the afternoon. I had almost half a day to explore Guwahati. While in Agartala, Pranjeet and I had talked a lot about the city.

My urine had turned yellow. Continuous travel and weather change was taking a toll on my health. My body was affected badly by dehydration. Somehow I managed to reach Siliguri and then boarded another bus to Patna.

It was early morning when I reached Patna. My train to Jabalpur was late in the night. I needed to freshen up and rest so I booked a room at a cheap lodge near the station. I took a shower and tried to sleep for a couple of hours, but bed bugs were biting me and I couldn't sleep properly. I had scars all over my body. The blanket smelled foul and looked very dirty.

I left for the station and just when my train started, I realized that I had forgotten to take my original PAN card from the reception. I hurriedly dialled Ravi's number and requested him to take it from the lodge. I hadn't told him that I would be in Patna and he was angry. Phew! Ten long minutes later I finally managed to convince him about my tight schedule.

*

One of my friends had connected me to Harsh, the eldest son of an Agarwal family in Jabalpur. Harsh headed the real estate division of his family business in construction and supplies. My job was to brainstorm with the publicity division of his firm for two of their upcoming projects. One was to build seventy duplex houses in the town, and the other was to construct a marriage garden.

Harsh's passion for theatre and art made him less of a businessperson and more of an artist. Before joining the family business, Harsh had worked with one of the leading theatre groups in Chennai. His creative approach was evident during meetings where we discussed the development of publicity for the projects. I was glad that I was not working with a typical real estate and construction company. People in these sectors are usually so money-driven and boring.

I visited the duplexes which had been designed especially for middle-class consumers. There were two types, one designed with a staircase in the middle while the other had a staircase on one of the sides. The latter was preferred as many middle-class families rented out the upper floor while they lived on the ground floor. I would make trips to the construction site every day. Harsh shared details about the profit margin difference between duplexes, singles, and flats.

The second project, the marriage garden, was a vision that would be the first of its kind in the city. The company's calculations indicated that the two main marriage seasons would easily cover the additional money they were investing in the project. Also, the success of the project would lead to a solid rise in the price of land in the neighbourhood and hence would hopefully invite better prospects for business. It is indeed true when people say that Marwaris have keen business sense.

During our talks, I noticed that Harsh was always scribbling something in a pocket diary. Later I learnt that he had a habit of taking notes about every new thing he heard. These habits of self-development are probably the signs that point towards the making of an industry leader.

Sonalal worked in Harsh's firm. A supervisor by day and Harsh's trusted assistant at other times, he hailed from Muzzafarabad district in Uttar Pradesh. It was my fourth day at work when I met him in Harsh's cabin. We had just returned from a field visit.

Sonalal's face was expressionless but I sensed that he was uneasy. I had only seen him around Harsh a few times but had not talked to him. He requested leave for a week as his father had passed away. His face remained the same, expressionless.

Earlier, Harsh had told me that Sonalal would show me around Jabalpur. Now that he was leaving for his village I planned to go alone.

*

Jabalpur, also called the *sanskaar dhaani* or cultural capital of Madhya Pradesh, was a beautiful city, but its roads were in very bad shape. Madhya Pradesh has a humid subtropical climate, typical of the northern part of central India. Winter had set in and it was dry.

Jabalpur is surrounded by low, rocky and barren hillocks. I had once visited a place called Gauri ghat, located on the banks of the Narmada. The water is dark greenish and the place as a whole feels very serene. Tourists would come in droves to take joy rides in boats painted in different colours.

It was my last week on the trip, and I felt a series of mixed emotions. Though extremely tired of changing places, my love for travel and life had only grown in the course of this journey.

I still had a day to complete my week at Harsh's firm. However, Harsh suggested that I take leave on my final day and visit Bedaghat. Famous for the Dhuandhar Falls, marble rocks and Chausanth Yogini temple, Bedaghat is a town located 20 kilometres from Jabalpur, situated on the banks of the Narmada.

The Chausanth Yogini temple bears carvings of 64 female mystics. These 64 postures relate to the art of seduction. Built in the tenth century by the Kalachuri rulers, the temple commands a view of the whole area around and of the river flowing through the marble rocks.

The Narmada makes its way through the world-famous marble rocks, narrows down and then plunges in a waterfall known as Dhuandhar. It is about 10 metres high. The plunge, which creates a lot of mist, is so powerful that its roar can be heard from a distance. *Dhuan* stands for smoke in Hindi and *dhar* for flow of water. The waterfall looks like smoke coming out of the river. It was the biggest waterfall I had ever seen. The waterfall had received national attention when Shahrukh Khan and Kareena Kapoor were pictured there in a scene in the movie *Ashoka*.

I hadn't expected to encounter such beauty in the last week of my journey. I would love to come back to Jabalpur one day to explore it further, I thought.

Epilogue

My train was from Jabalpur to Raipur, from where I would take another train and a bus to reach home. But on the way, I could not wait till Raipur so I decided to take one more train from Bilaspur, which would reduce my journey by six hours. I got down from the train in Bilaspur and reached my hometown via Jharsuguda and Sambalpur.

The best part of my hometown, Sonepur, is the bridge that one has to cross to enter from either side. By the time I reached, the stars were twinkling in the sky. A stranger passing by offered me a lift, but I wanted to walk. It was a full moon night. Cold wind bent the grass as frogs starting croaking on that blustery December night. The familiar smell of my land hung in the air. I looked up and smiled.

Life is indeed a journey. Letting go of Sameen had been tough but I had accepted that we could not be together again. Things had changed. Now, thoughts of her would no longer pain me, though she would always occupy a special place in my heart.

The next morning, I woke up in a warm bed after a long time. The soft linen blanket I had brought from Shillong gave me a cosy feeling. My mother was in the kitchen, calling me for breakfast. I looked at the old oval clock. It was nine in the morning. The bright rays of the morning sun were peeking through the gaps in the curtains that hung over the window, falling on my face. A sudden fear froze me, but then it melted away when the realization struck: I had no trains to catch.

While clearing up my bags and laptop, a whole flashback of the last seven to eight months of 2013 hit me. The bus tickets from different states, train tatkal moments, ILP passes, movie tickets, medicine strips, chocolate wrappers from China Bazaar in Kolkata, empty chips packet from Goa, visiting cards from every corner of the country, write-ups, important mail docs, photos which I can't post on FB , newspaper screenshots, oldies songs, a few songs in different Indian languages I had heard for the first time, movies I had collected, notepads scribbled with short notes and new ideas, weekly job reports, unpublished articles and some best left unpublished. It was time to look at all those and my notes, to refresh my memory, and write it all down in the form of a book.

I had travelled a total distance of around 25,000 kilometres across the country by all possible modes of transport: train, bus, share taxi, airplane, tram, auto rikshaw, bike, cab, boat, raft, and obviously, on foot. As per my plan, I had stayed in hotel rooms that had ranged from 120 to 500 rupees maximum per night. My favourite room was in Darjeeling which cost me 250 rupees and offered a beautiful sunrise view from the balcony. Even sleeping under a banyan tree during my week in Bihar was memorable.

I had been passionate about my One Week Job project

of '28 Jobs, 28 Weeks, 28 States'. After completing the whole journey I was feeling confident and very happy. I had set out prepared to do any kind of menial jobs, which really happened while cleaning mountains, in cremation ghats and selling peanuts while jobless in Chennai. It started out as a journey to self-discovery and concluded with the satisfaction of completing a challenge I had set myself.

Before I started my journey, I knew little about the north-eastern states of India. I neither had friends nor any contacts over there. But when I look back I made some really good friends in Gangtok, Imphal and Aizwal. Travel opens the mind and gives you the opportunity to make good friends in different parts of the world.

Here are some quick tips that I picked up through the course of my journey. You always find people who are well informed even in unexpected places. A good storyteller makes your journey smooth. You never know in which part of country you start feeling like you're at home. I didn't expect to but I found flora and fauna in Manipur which was similar to that in Odisha. Bollywood songs are an integral part of every Indian, and you'll hear familiar tunes whether while passing through the beautiful Himalayas or in local transport in central India. There is no point feeling proud of reaching a remote place with tents, expensive cameras and bikes—the civilization that still exists there goes back a thousand years or more.

With an engineering degree, a good management school degree, work experience and a family I could fall back on, I had taken a calculated risk with this seven-month trip. It turned out be the experience of a lifetime.

In Gratitude

The truth is I have earned more friends than money.

A big thank you to my crowdfunding supporters who helped me raise 102,000 rupees to meet the expenses of this '28 Jobs, 28 Weeks, 28 States' journey.

Rahul Narvekar, Abhishek Mahapatra

Ajay Sethi, Milind Katti, Abhiram Padhi

Manish Chaudhary, Leena Bansal, Soumyo Das, Jagdish Sahu, R Sashikanth, Imran Ansari

Chirag Rathod, Khitish Mishra, Pradeep Sahoo, Viswanath Kapuganti, Om Prakash Rout, Deepika RN, Swadhin Bohidar, Anil Maharana, Abhishek Shekhar Choudhary, Jeeth Mathew Eapen, Manish Agrawal, Paromita Panda, Nimesh Shah, Pritiman Panda, Seshagiri Dama, Suzoy Banerjiee, Somojyoti Biswal, Sandeep Hotta, Falguni Vasavada, Atul Jain, Mukesh Panda, Biswajit Behera, Biranchi Kumar Parhi, Abhash Kumar, Shakti Prasad Misra, Pratyush Panda, Alok Prusty, Pritam Kumar Sahu, Kuldip Mitra, Sudeep Behera, Sarat Kumar Parsan

Asit Kumar Das, Abhishek Bhattacharya, Sujit Samantaray, Subrato Biswas, Aparajita Mishra, Prem Nepak, Jayanti

Rath, Ashutosh Behera, Hari Haran, Soubhagya Mishra, Tripati Patro, Bishnu Panda, Navdeep Aggarwal, Kamlesh Parida, Nayanansu Mishra, Vikram Mishra, Devidutta Ratha, Swati Dwivedi, Sailekha Mishra, Piyush Panda, Vaibhav Jha, Abhishek Kumar, Neha Srivastava, Gaurav Upadhyay, Vyas Bhandari, Subhranshu Mishra, Tejas Vora, Sanjay Kumar Behera, Asem Roshni Chanu, Pavan Ghatge, Ankur Bakshi, Pallab Rath, Bimalendu Behera, Ashok Kumar Swain, Sudipta Chowdhury, Pradeep Dash, Samir Tarai, Ankita Shrivastava, Paulomi Mukherjee, Aditi Gupta